Real Talk 1
Authentic English in Context

Lida Baker
Judith Tanka

PEARSON
Longman

Real Talk 1

Pearson Education, 10 Bank Street, White Plains, NY 10606

Staff credits: The people who made up the *Real Talk 1* team, representing editorial, production, design, and manufacturing, are Elizabeth Carlson, Christine Edmonds, Nancy Flaggman, Laura Lazzaretti, Laura Le Dréan, Molly Sackler, and Paula Van Ells.

Text composition: Laserwords
Text font: 11.5/13 Minon Regular
Text art: Barbara Sabella
Illustrations: Paul Hampson

Text and audio credits: Page 22, Interview with Mary Newton Bruder, on WordMaster, August 29, 2002. Used with permission from Voice of America. **Page 38**, The Savvy Traveler: Traveler Update segments from 8/16/97, 8/30/97, 9/27/97, and 2/7/98 © 1997, 1998, 2000, Minnesota Public Radio. All rights reserved. Reproduced with permission of Minnesota Public Radio (www.mpr.org) and American Public Media. **Page 65**, "Living Single," Morning Edition, 6/25/02, © National Public Radio Incorporated. Used with permission. **Page 88**, "College Students Shrug at Threats over File-Sharing," 6/29/03, Weekend Edition © National Public Radio Incorporated. Used with permission. **Page 115**, "Workplace Etiquette" on MarketPlace®, (interview with Peggy and Peter Post), 9/4/00 © 1997, 1998, 2000, Minnesota Public Radio. All rights reserved. Reproduced with permission of Minnesota Public Radio (www.mpr.org) and American Public Media. Marketplace® is the largest daily national business show and is heard on over 330 public radio stations. Visit Marketplace on the web at www.marketplace.org. **Page 142**, "Obesity No Longer Just a US Problem," by Stephanie Ho, August 28, 2003. Used with permission from Voice of America. **Page 168**, "Shoppers Panic in a Sea of Choice," Morning Edition, 12/2/03, © National Public Radio Incorporated. **Page 195**, Originally broadcast June 12, 2002 on CBC radio program "As It Happens" © Canadian Broadcasting Corporation. Used with permission.

Photo credits: Page 8, left, © Dex Images/Corbis. **Page 8**, right, © Rob Lewine/Corbis, **Page 28**, top, © Fotosearch. **Page 28**, middle, © age fotostock/ Superstock. **Page 28**, bottom, © Peter Beck/Corbis. **Page 34**, © Michael Newman/Photo Edit. **Page 50**, left, © Photodisc Green/Getty Images. **Page 50**, right, © Pierre Perrin/Corbis Sygma. **Page 51**, © Jutta Klee/Corbis. **Page 63**, left, © Taxi/Getty Images. **Page 63**, right, © Royalty-Free/Corbis. **Page 76**, © Richard Aaron/Getty Images. **Page 85**, © S.I.N./Corbis. **Page 87**, © Jutta Klee/Corbis. **Page 92**, © Jo Hale/Stringer/2004 Getty Images. **Page 108**, © Royalty-Free/Corbis. **Page 128**, top, © Digital Vision/Getty Image. **Page 128**, bottom, © Photodisc Blue/Getty Images. **Page 141**, left, © Dex Image/Fotosearch. **Page 141**, right, © Photodisc/Fotosearch. **Page 145**, © Comstock Images. **Page 165**, © Royalty-Free/Corbis. **Page 166**, © Royalty-Free/Corbis. **Page 172**, © Photofest. **Page 175**, © Photofest. **Page 179**, © Chuck Savage/Corbis. **Page 188**, photo by Judith Tanka, with permission of the UCLA police department. **Page 189**, © Index Stock/Fotosearch. **Page 193**, © Taxi/Getty. **Page 195**, © Image Source/Fotosearch.

Library of Congress Cataloging-in-Publication Data

Baker, Lida R.
  Real Talk 1/ Lida Baker and Judith Tanka.
    p. cm.
  Summary: Real Talk 1 is an English language learning textbook that uses authentic listening passages in a variety of genuine contexts as the basis for listening and speaking skills development. The book is designed for students at the high intermediate level in both second- and foreign-language environments.
  Includes bibliographical references and index.
  ISBN 0-13-183545-9 (student book : alk. paper) -- ISBN 0-13-194547-5 (audio CD program) -- ISBN 0-13-194554-8 (teacher's manual : alk. paper)
  1. English language--Textbooks for foreign speakers. 2. English language--Spoken English--Problems, exercises, etc. 3. Listening--Problems, exercises, etc. I. Tanka, Judith, 1950- II. Title.
PE1128.B273 2006
428.3'4--dc22

2005013872

ISBN: 0-13-183545-9

Printed in the United States of America
2 3 4 5 6 7 8 9 10–VHG–10 09 08 07 06

CONTENTS

DEDICATION

We dedicate this book to all the family members, friends, and colleagues who so generously shared their time and vocal talents with us.

SPECIAL THANKS

We would like to express our special thanks to the outstanding team of professionals at Pearson Longman. It has been a joy working with you.

ACKNOWLEDGMENTS

We thank the following people who were instrumental in making this book:

Dan Abatelli
David Ackerman
Ellen Ackerman
Dr. Misha Askren
Joyce Baker
Bob Baldwin
Mark Burbonnaise
Bonnie Cheeseman
Jean Cox
Andrea Domanick
Joe Domanick
Kyle Duncan
Benjamin Eisenbise
Jonathan Epstein
Bene Ferrao
Bruce Fogel

Laura Gover
Cheryl Hersch
Rena Horowitz
Stephannie Howard
Kurt Kainsinger
Ilana Kellerman
Spencer Krul
Nira Kvart
Katherine Lee
Bonnie Leib
Sarah Leib
Mark Mabray
David Mannheim
Paul Martella
Brenda Means
Nikki McGee

Lisa Mikesell
Karen Muldoon-Hules
Tara Neuwirth
Susie Nicholson
Tim Norton
Lisa Patriquin-Esmaili
Carmen Piccini
Gena Pilic
Kathleen Schulweiss
Erik Severson
Melinda Smith
Phaidra Speirs
Felipe Tetelboin
Michael Thomas
Alia Yunis

SCOPE AND SEQUENCE

	Speaking Skills	
	Conversation Tools (Vocabulary and Functions)	**Focus on Sound (Pronunciation)**
CHAPTER 1: WHAT'S IN A NAME?	• Talking about names • Using fillers • Using titles and forms of address	• Sentence stress • Stress on negative words
CHAPTER 2 LET'S GET AWAY!	• Expressing annoyance • Giving advice	• Linking
CHAPTER 3 LOOKING FOR LOVE	• Interrupting • Expressing doubt or uncertainty • Love idioms	• Reductions • Word stress for emphasis
CHAPTER 4 MUSIC TO MY EARS	• Adjectives for describing music	• Stress in compound nouns • Stress in phrasal verbs
CHAPTER 5 GETTING THE JOB DONE	• Expressing surprise, interest, amusement • Asking, granting, or denying permission • Checking for consensus	• Intonation of questions, unfinished thoughts, hesitations
CHAPTER 6 TO YOUR HEALTH!	• Expressing sympathy • Expressing worry and reassurance • Reporting verbs and phrases	• Thought groups and focus words: stress and pauses
CHAPTER 7 SHOP 'TIL YOU DROP	• Idioms for talking about prices	• Reductions: unstressed vowels and dropped *h* • Intonation of questions • American flapped *t*
CHAPTER 8 DO THE RIGHT THING	• Expressing disbelief • Signaling imaginary situations • Idioms for telling truth and lies	• Reduced unreal conditionals • Review of stress and linking in phrasal verbs

Listening Skills	Note-Taking Skills
• **Understanding main ideas and details** • **Inferring relationships**	• Identifying the features of good notes: abbreviations, key words, indentation • Taking notes on statistics
• **Using introductions to predict content** • **Inferring attitudes** • **Recognizing definitions** • Understanding main ideas and details	• Understanding the importance of lecture introductions • Defining terms
• **Using voice cues** • **Identifying reasons** • Understanding main ideas and details	• Recognizing and noting transitions in lectures • Outlining
• **Recognizing the connotation of adjectives** • **Recognizing paraphrase** • Understanding main ideas and details	• Classifying • Paraphrasing
• **Using intonation cues to recognize emotions** • **Recognizing the purpose of a phone call** • Understanding main ideas and details • Inferring	• Organizing and noting causes and effects
• Understanding main ideas and details • Inferring	• Organizing and noting comparisons and contrasts
• Understanding main ideas and details • Inferring	• Taking notes on arguments pro and con
• Understanding main ideas and details • Inferring	• Recognizing rhetorical questions • Recognizing digressions

TO THE TEACHER

Real Talk 1 is a program that uses authentic listening segments in a variety of genuine contexts as the basis for listening and speaking skills development. The book is designed for students at the intermediate to high-intermediate level in both second- and foreign-language environments.

This book differs from most other listening/speaking books in two important ways. First, the listening material consists of recordings of "real" people (not actors) speaking in four contexts: in person, on the phone, on the air, and in class. The recordings retain all the false starts, fillers, hesitations, repetitions, and errors that are an integral part of authentic English. By means of carefully structured and sequenced exercises, the book teaches students how to identify the essential information in the imperfect and disorganized stream of sound they often encounter in real English-speaking contexts.

In addition, *Real Talk 1* is unusual in its organization. The book consists of eight theme-based chapters, each of which is divided into four parts named after the four contexts above, that is, **In Person, On the Phone, On the Air**, and **In Class**. Each of these parts has a listening passage as its centerpiece. To give an example, Chapter 2, *Let's Get Away!*, is about travel. This topic is developed in four different ways:

- *In Person* features people talking about their travel pet peeves.

- *On the Phone* presents a recorded phone conversation between a client and a travel agent.

- *On the Air* has a series of travel advisories from a radio program called *The Savvy Traveler.*

- *In Class* presents a mini-lecture about the fear of flying.

Each chapter part is divided into prelistening, listening, and post-listening sections:

Prelistening. This section includes:

- a vocabulary preview exercise

- a speaking activity in which students explore their existing knowledge and attitudes about the theme of the listening.

Listening. This section includes the following listening comprehension activities, each of which aids in the development of a different set of listening skills:

- *Main Ideas*: Global listening requiring top-down processing.

- *Details and Inferences*: Listening for specific information and synthesizing details for the purpose of drawing conclusions, respectively. This exercise encourages both bottom-up and top-down processing.

- *Listening for Language*: Structure-based, bottom-up activities presented under the headings *Focus on Sound*, which deals with phonological features of English, and *Conversation Tools*, which presents situation-based vocabulary ("notions") and language for specific communicative functions, such as apologizing, requesting permission, etc. As an example, in Chapter 6, *To Your Health*, a young woman tells a friend that she had to give up her cat because of her allergies. The friend responds sympathetically. "Expressing sympathy" then becomes one of the teaching points of this section.

The Listening section in part four of every chapter, *In Class*, features activities targeting lecture form, organization, and language.

Post-listening. Called *Real Talk! Use What You've Learned*, this section includes a vocabulary review and one or more communicative speaking activities that incorporate the skills and language presented in the previous two sections.

Although we recommend covering the chapters in order, it is not essential to teach every chapter of **Real Talk 1**, nor is it necessary to cover all four parts of every chapter. The parts are sufficiently self-contained that you may choose among them according to the needs and interests of your students. Because most of the activities involve students working in pairs or groups, we think the book is best suited to classroom use.

The audio program consists of a set of three CDs. A Teacher's Manual containing answers to exercises, teaching suggestions, and eight chapter tests covering the vocabulary and other language presented in each chapter is also available.

We hope that you and your students will enjoy using **Real Talk 1**!

L. B. and J. T.

TO THE STUDENT

What kind of book is this?

Have you ever been frustrated because English in the real world is much harder to understand than English in your classroom or your textbook? We have created *Real Talk 1* to help you bridge that gap. *Real Talk 1* offers you a unique opportunity to listen to authentic recordings in the four contexts where you are most likely to hear and use English: in person, on the phone, on the air (radio), and in class.

How is each chapter organized?

Each of the eight chapters deals with a general theme such as relationships, travel, health, etc. Chapters are then divided into four parts, called *In Person, On the Phone, On the Air,* and *In Class.* Each of these parts has its own authentic listening passage and a variety of activities. These include:

- speaking and vocabulary activities to get you ready for listening.
- listening activities focusing on comprehension of main ideas, details, inferences, on pronunciation and on language functions.
- exercises to help you learn and practice note-taking.
- vocabulary review and communicative speaking activities to practice the vocabulary and the language skills taught in that part.

What do you mean by authentic recordings?

The recordings for this book were not produced with actors in a studio. For *In Person* and *On the Phone,* we recorded "real" people—our friends, family members, colleagues, and even strangers in the street—talking about high-interest, contemporary topics. *On the Air* uses radio segments selected for their relevance and usefulness to adult learners of English. These recordings have been shortened but not simplified. *In Class* features mini-lectures delivered and recorded in front of an audience of students at the American Language Center, UCLA Extension.

What about speaking activities?

There are opportunities to practice speaking in every part of every chapter. Most activities involve your working with a partner or in small groups. One of the unique features of the book, called *Conversation Tools,* presents lists of expressions you can use for specific purposes, such as interrupting, apologizing, and many more. In this way the book helps you to develop your speaking, as well as listening, skills.

Whatever your purpose is for learning English (academic, personal or professional), we hope *Real Talk 1* will help you to improve your ability to understand and communicate with speakers of North American English.

1

What's in a Name?

Part One: In Person

A. Prelistening

DISCUSSION

You will hear a conversation about names. Before you listen, discuss the following question with a partner or in a small group.

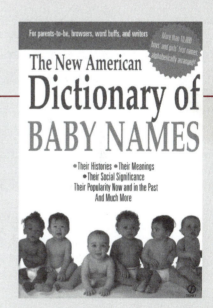

- What are some ways that people get their first names, family names, and nicknames in different cultures?

Examples: Many English family names are names of professions, such as *Baker, Cooper,* and *Smith.*

VOCABULARY PREVIEW

Read the sentences. Using the context, guess the meanings of the boldfaced words and expressions. Then match them with their definitions. You will hear this vocabulary in the conversation.

1. _____ In Chinese names, the last name always comes first. This doesn't **make sense** to some English-speakers.

2. _____ My name is Theodore Travis Norton, but my **nickname** has always been Theo.

3. _____ There are only four people in my **immediate family**, but I have dozens of aunts, uncles, and cousins.

4. _____ What was your parents' **reaction** when you told them you wanted to change your name? Were they angry?

5. _____ My family name is more than 500 years old. It goes back to **medieval** times in Germany.

6. _____ One of my **ancestors** on my mother's side was a Spanish prince who lived 200 years ago.

7. _____ In the Middle Ages, **knights** fought with swords while riding on horseback. They wore suits made of metal.

---

a. European soldiers who fought on horseback centuries ago

b. family members who lived in past times

c. have a clear meaning and be easy to understand

d. a silly name or a shorter form of someone's real name

e. mother, father, sisters, and brothers

f. a feeling or action in response to a situation or question

g. relating to the Middle Ages in Europe (about A.D. 500–1500)

B. Listening

MAIN IDEAS

🎧 **1** Listen to two friends, Alia and Benjamin, talk about their names. Check (✓) the name of the person(s) that each statement describes.

	Alia	Benjamin
1. Has a Lebanese name		
2. Has a nickname		
3. Has a very common last name		
4. Has an unusual last name		
5. Family name means "iron bite"		

2 Now work with a classmate and compare answers.

DETAILS AND INFERENCES

🎧 **3** Listen again and answer the questions.

1. Alia's first name

   a. is the Arabic word for "whale."

   b. came from an Arabic love story.

   c. is pronounced "Jonah."

2. Alia's brother is _____ she is.

   a. older than

   b. the same age as

   c. younger than

3. Alia's family name

   a. means "whale."

   b. is English.

   c. is very common in Arabic.

4. Ben thinks "Benjamin" is

    a. too formal.

    b. too hard to pronounce.

    c. too common.

5. Ben learned about the story of his last name

    a. when he was a child.

    b. recently.

    c. from Alia.

6. Alia thinks _____ is "cool."

    a. Ben's nickname

    b. the fact that Ben's ancestors were Bavarian knights

    c. the fact that Ben found his name on the Internet

7. Bavaria is in

    a. Lebanon.

    b. the United States.

    c. Germany.

8. Shield _____ shows Ben's family shield.

a.   b.   c.

LISTENING FOR LANGUAGE

 ④ Read the information about sentence stress. Then listen to part of the conversation. Pay attention to sentence stress.

FOCUS ON SOUND
Sentence Stress

In English, words that convey important information in a sentence are usually stressed. This means they are pronounced more clearly and at a higher pitch than other words in the sentence. Understanding English stress is a very important part of improving your listening and speaking skills.

- The following "content" words are usually stressed: nouns, verbs, adjectives, adverbs ending in -ly, negative words, question words, and numbers.

- The following "function" words are usually not stressed: to be verbs, helping verbs, articles, prepositions, conjunctions, and pronouns.

- A speaker may choose to stress any word in the sentence in order to emphasize it.

⑤ Listen again. Fill in the missing stressed words during the pauses.

Ben: So did you say that your _____ is thirteen

_____ younger than you?

Alia: No, thirteen _____ .

Ben: OK, _____ 3 _____ makes more _____ .

Ben: And what about your _____ name, Alia? "Yunis" is your last

name? 6

Alia: Yeah.

Ben: What does _____ mean?

Alia: It's a super- _____ 7 _____ name in Arabic. In

_____ , it literally means _____ . Uh, Jonah who

got _____ 9 _____ by the _____ 10 _____ in the

_____ 11 _____ ? 12

Ben: Oh, yeah. I _____ that _____ .

14 15

6 Read the conversation with a partner. Remember to pronounce the stressed words clearly and at a higher pitch.

7 Read the questions and answers in the chart below. These examples will help you talk about names.

CONVERSATION TOOLS

Talking about Names

What is your **first name**?	My **first name** is Benjamin.
What is your **last (family) name**?	My **last (family) name** is Eisenbise.
What is your **middle name**?	I don't have a **middle name**.
Do you have a **nickname**?	Yes, my **nickname** is Ben.
Who **named** you?	My parents **named** me.
Who were you **named after (for)**?	I was named **after (for)** my grandfather.
What does your name **mean**?	Eisenbise **means** "iron bite."
What do people **call** you?	People **call** me Ben.
What should I **call** you?	Please **call** me Ben.
What do you like **to be called**?	I like **to be called** Ben.

8 Work with a partner. Interview each other about your names and fill in the chart. Use examples from the chart above. If your partner cannot answer a question, leave the space blank.

Partner's first name
Origin / reason for name _____

Meaning _____

Partner's middle name
Origin / reason for name _____

Meaning _____

Partner's last (family) name
Origin / reason for name _____

Meaning _____

Partner's nickname
Origin / reason for name _____

Meaning _____

9 Now work with a different classmate. Use your notes to tell each other about the person you interviewed in Exercise 8.

C. Real Talk: Use What You've Learned

VOCABULARY REVIEW: DISCUSSION

Work with a partner or a small group. Discuss the questions below. Use the Part One vocabulary from the box. Remember to stress important words and phrases.

ancestors	make sense	reaction
immediate family	nickname	

1. How many people are there in your immediate family? Tell their names and a little bit about each person.
2. What country, city, or village did your ancestors come from? Do you know anything about their names or history?
3. What are some popular names in your culture, country, or religion?
4. What are the advantages and disadvantages of having an unusual name?
5. Is your name common or unusual?
6. Do you believe children's names can influence their personality or their chance for success later in life?
7. Did you ever have a nickname you disliked? What was your reaction when people used that nickname?

ROLE PLAY

Work in pairs. Follow these steps.

1. Find information about a celebrity who changed his or her name. (For example, did you know that Elton John's real name is Reginald Dwight?) Search the Internet using key words or terms such as *celebrity real names*, *stage names*, or *pen names*.
2. Make a list of questions a reporter will ask a famous person who changed his or her name. Role play a two- to three-minute interview. One student is the famous person. The other is the reporter.

   Example:

   Reporter: When did you change your name to Elton John?

   Elton John: I changed it when I decided to become a singer.

   Reporter: Why? Didn't you like your own name?

   Elton John: Well, actually, it was my manager's idea.

3. Switch roles.

INTERVIEW AN ENGLISH SPEAKER

If possible, repeat Exercise 8 on page 6 with an English speaker. First write the questions you will ask. Interview the person and take detailed notes. Then come back to class and tell a partner about the person you interviewed.

Part Two: On the Phone

A. Prelistening

DISCUSSION

You will hear a phone conversation about names. Before you listen, discuss the following question with a partner or in a small group.

- Do you know anyone who has changed his or her name? How and why did the person do it?

VOCABULARY PREVIEW

Read the sentences. Using the context, guess the meanings of the boldfaced words and expressions. Then match them with their definitions. You will hear this vocabulary in the conversation. (*Note*: All the expressions are *informal*.)

1. _____ Hi, Jason. **What's up**?

2. _____ I can't **get started** on this homework until I find my textbook and notes.

3. _____ I'm **sick of** working in an office every day. It's so boring. I want to travel more.

4. _____ Tim **can't stand** his middle name, so he never tells anyone what it is.

5. _____ A **bunch of** people called while you were on vacation. You have twenty-five messages.

6. _____ Getting information from the government is sometimes easy, but often it's a **hassle**.

7. _____ Ten minutes before the wedding, the bride changed her mind and decided not to **go through with it**.

8. _____ I've **got to run**; I'm late for a meeting.

---

a. need to leave quickly

b. complete something unpleasant or difficult

c. an unpleasant and difficult task

d. What's new? What do you want?

e. begin

f. hates

g. tired of, impatient with

h. a large number of

B. Listening

MAIN IDEAS

Listen to two friends talk on the phone about changing names. Write brief answers to the questions. Then work with a partner and compare answers.

1. Why does Reka want to talk to Judy?

_____

2. What is Reka thinking about doing?

_____

3. How does Reka feel about her last name? Why?

_____

4. Where did Judy go to change her name?

_____

DETAILS AND INFERENCES

 2 Listen again. Mark the statements *T* (true) or *F* (false).

_____ 1. The women have not seen each other recently.

_____ 2. Judy is going through a divorce.

_____ 3. Judy paid a lot of money to change her name.

_____ 4. Judy had no trouble changing her name.

_____ 5. Reka has been working for a large company.

_____ 6. Reka's last name is long.

_____ 7. Reka is definitely going to change her name.

LISTENING FOR LANGUAGE

Read the information about stress on negative words.

FOCUS ON SOUND
Stress on Negative Words

Like content words, negative words are usually stressed. It is common for a phrase or sentence to have several stressed words. For example:

- Judy doesn't like her name.
- Alia has never been to Lebanon.
- I can't hear you.
- Jay doesn't have any money.

🎧 **4** Listen to sentences from the conversation. Underline the stressed words. Then repeat each sentence during the pause.

1. I don't remember what it cost . . .

2. Probably not very much . . .

3. . . . don't laugh, OK, I really can't stand my last name!

4. You never told me that!

5. I'm not ready to tell anybody yet.

6. Sure, no problem. Great. I'll talk to you soon, Reka.

5 Read the information about conversation fillers.

CONVERSATION TOOLS
Recognizing and Using Fillers

Many English-speakers are not comfortable with long silences in a conversation. For that reason, English speech is full of "fillers." Fillers are sounds or words that don't have any meaning. Their purpose is to give a speaker time to think about what he or she wants to say next. Look at this example from the conversation:

Reka: Well, **um,** there's a question that I've been meaning to ask you for a while. **Um,** I remember that you changed your name a few years ago, after your divorce, **right,** and **um** . . . I—I wanted to know how you did it. **I mean** legally, **you know,** how you changed your name legally.

Judy: Oh. Um, gee, that was three years ago already. **OK. Well,** all I remember is that I had to go downtown and fill out a bunch of forms.

Notice that the fillers can be deleted, but the meaning does not change. Here is a list of common fillers:

hmmm . . .	like . . .	um . . .
I mean . . .	so . . .	well . . .
let me see . . .	uh . . .	you know . . .

6 Imagine a phone call Reka makes to the courthouse to get information about changing names. With a partner, take the roles of Reka and the courthouse clerk. Create a conversation using the information below. Try to use fillers from Exercise 5.

Begin like this:

Reka: Hello. I'm calling to find out about name changes. Uh, what do I need to do, I mean, where can I get a legal name change?

Clerk: Well, first, you have to . . .

REKA

Get information about:

- where you need to go
- what forms to fill out
- the cost of a name change
- how long it takes

CLERK

Answer Reka's questions using this information:

- Courthouse: 111 North Hill Street, corner of Hill and First streets, downtown
- Fill out forms in "Name-change application packet," available in room 112
- Cost: $194 filing fee
- Takes six to eight weeks

7 Now role play your dialogue for another pair of students in your class.

C. Real Talk: Use What You've Learned

VOCABULARY REVIEW: DESCRIBING PICTURES

Work with a partner or in a small group. Use Part Two vocabulary from the box below to describe what the people in the pictures on the next page might be thinking or saying.

sick of	can't stand	go through with (something)	I've got to run
a bunch of	get started	a hassle	What's up?

A.

B.

C.

D.

DISCUSSION

Work in small groups. Discuss the questions. Add your own comments and questions. If you need time to think about what you want to say, use fillers during the silence.

1. In your culture, can you change your first or last name legally if you want to? Who would you call to find out how to do this?

2. If you had a chance, would you choose a different name for yourself? Why or why not?

Part Three: On The Air

A. Prelistening

DISCUSSION

1. You will hear a radio interview about formal and informal ways to address people in English. Before listening, discuss the following questions with a partner or in a small group.

   • Does your language have both formal and informal ways to address people?

   • Do you know formal and informal ways to address people in English?

   • What words do English speakers use to address people whose names they don't know?

2. The following sentences were spoken to a woman named Kathy Lynn Thomas. Discuss who the speakers might be and why you think so. Take notes on your answers.

Sentences	Relationship		The speaker is probably . . .
	Formal	Informal	
1. Hey, Kathy, how are you doing?		✓	a friend, knows her well
2. I'm sorry, Ms. Thomas, the results of the test aren't ready yet.			
3. Do you have the time, ma'am?			
4. Ma, are you picking me up from soccer practice today?			
5. Dr. Thomas, I really need to talk to you.			

VOCABULARY PREVIEW

Read the sentences. Using the context, guess the meanings of the boldfaced words and expressions. Then match them with their definitions. You will hear this vocabulary in the interview.

1. _____ Children should be polite when they **address** their teachers.

2. _____ *Doctor* and *Professor* are common **titles** for teachers at universities.

3. _____ When English speakers talk quickly, some listeners can't **differentiate** between *Ms.* and *Mrs.*

4. _____ Because she has loved languages from an early age, she decided to become a **linguist**.

5. _____ Our French teacher, Madame Beaujolais, gave us **explicit** instructions regarding the proper pronunciation of her name.

6. _____ The college's admissions counselors interviewed **prospective** students after reviewing their applications.

7. _____ English speakers often use the terms *sir* and *ma'am* when speaking to someone **in authority**, such as an employer.

8. _____ In most situations it is rude to call older people by their first names **unless** you ask for permission first.

9. _____ By the end of the first day of the conference, everybody started to **loosen up**; they began using each others' first names.

---

a. except on the condition that; except if

b. likely to happen; future (*adj.*)

c. having the power and right to control and command people

d. words or names that describe someone's rank or position

e. speak directly to a person or group

f. a person who studies languages and their structures

g. become more relaxed and feel less worried

h. recognize the differences among various things or people

i. expressed in a way that is very clear

B. Listening

MAIN IDEAS

🎧 ① Listen to an interview with linguist Mary Newton Bruder. She explains some formal and informal ways of addressing people in the United States. Complete the rules.

1. If you want to be very formal with people you've just met, use their _____ plus their _____.

2. If you want to be less formal, use their _____.

3. If you don't know the name of a woman, call her _____ or _____.

4. If you are meeting a prospective employer or a person in authority, use his or her _____.

DETAILS AND INFERENCES

② Read the following information about inferences.

INFERRING

When listening to people, you can learn a lot of information not only from what they say *directly* but also from what they say *indirectly*. Guessing from indirect information is called "inferring." Inferring is an important part of listening.

Example:

Direct information: The phone is ringing but nobody is picking up.
Inference: They are probably not home.

🎧 ③ Listen to part of the interview again. Which statements can be inferred from the information? Write *Yes* or *No*.

_____ 1. College students don't use *sir* and *ma'am* very often.

_____ 2. Formality varies from region to region in the United States.

_____ 3. The young college student doesn't know Roseanne's first name.

_____ 4. Roseanne is probably not from the South.

_____ 5. If you want to be very formal and polite, call a man *sir*.

4 Review your responses in Exercise 3 with a classmate. What information helped you infer the answers?

LISTENING FOR LANGUAGE

5 Read the information about titles and forms of address.

CONVERSATION TOOLS
Titles and Forms of Address

To avoid misunderstandings in formal situations, it is important to use titles and forms of address correctly.

Generally, if you know a person's name, use his or her title and name.

Example: "How are you, **Ms.** Brown?"

If you don't know a person's name but want to show respect, use *Miss, ma'am,* or *sir.*

Example: "Excuse me, **ma'am.** Do you know the time?"

Title and Pronunciation	To Address
Mrs. (*misiz*) + family name	a married woman
Miss (*mis*) + family name	an unmarried woman
Ms. (*miz*) + family name	a married or unmarried woman
Mister (*mister*) + family name	a man
Miss (*mis*) + no name	a younger woman whose name you do not know
Ma'am (*mam*) + no name	an older woman or a woman in a position of authority
Sir (*ser*) + no name	an older man or a man in a position of authority

6 Listen to the sentences and circle the title you hear.

1. Mr.   Ms.   Miss   Mrs.
2. Mr.   Ms.   Miss   Mrs.
3. Mr.   Ms.   Miss   Mrs.
4. Mr.   Ms.   Miss   Mrs.
5. Mr.   Ms.   Miss   Mrs.
6. Mr.   Ms.   Miss   Mrs.

C. Real Talk: Use What You've Learned

VOCABULARY REVIEW: DISCUSSION

Work in pairs or small groups. Discuss the following questions. Remember to use the Part Three vocabulary in the box.

address	in authority	prospective
differentiate	linguist	titles
explicit	loosen up	unless

1. In your culture, what titles do you use to address people in authority, such as your teacher, employer, an older relative, or a police officer?
2. Does your language differentiate between married and unmarried names? Are there explicit rules?
3. Do people ever refuse to marry someone because of his or her name? How important is a prospective spouse's family name?
4. After people from your culture meet, does their language change as they begin to loosen up with one another?

ROLE PLAY

Role play one of the following situations with a partner. Pay special attention to formal and informal uses of names and titles.

1. Roles: A student and a teacher in an English program

Student:

Make an appointment with your English teacher. Her name is Janice Houston. She is single. Explain why and when you want to meet with her. Be very polite and formal.

> Teacher:
>
> Your name is Janice Houston. Your are an English teacher. A student wants to make an appointment with you. She is very formal, but you prefer a more informal style. Give her permission to call you by your first name.

2. Roles: Two new neighbors

> Neighbor 1:
>
> You want to meet your new American neighbor, who lives next door to you . Walk up and start a conversation by introducing yourself. Tell the neighbor what you prefer to be called. Find out the following about your neighbor:
> - name
> - when he or she moved in
> - how he or she likes the area
> - where he or she moved from

> Neighbor 2:
>
> You just moved into a new neighborhood three days ago. A friendly neighbor whom you never met before starts a conversation with you. Be friendly and informal. Find out the following about your neighbor:
> - name
> - which house or apartment he or she lives in
> - how long he or she has lived there
> - recommendations about restaurants, markets, or places to shop
> - entertainment in the area

3. Roles: A job applicant and a manager's assistant

Job Applicant:

You had a job interview a week ago with a woman named Maggie Flowers. Call her up to find out if you got the job or not. She is not available to speak with you on the phone, so leave a message with her assistant. Tell the reason you called and where and when Ms. Flowers can reach you.

Manager's Assistant:

Your boss interviewed some applicants for a job. One of the applicants calls and wants to speak to your boss, Maggie Flowers. Ms. Flowers is not available right now, so take a message for her. Find out why the applicant is calling and where and when she can be reached. Be polite and formal.

Part Four: In Class

A. Prelistening

DISCUSSION

You will hear a lecture about women who decide not to change their family names when they get married. Before listening, discuss the following questions with a partner or in a small group.

1. Read the wedding announcement. What is the husband's name?

2. What is the wife's name? Is this usual or unusual, in your opinion?

> *THE NEW YORK GAZETTE*
>
> **WEDDINGS/CELEBRATIONS**
>
> *DECEMBER 7, 2005*
>
> ### Martha Jude Cox, John Wakesfield
>
> Dr. Martha Jude Cox, the daughter of Elena and Steven J. Cox, was married yesterday to John Wakesfield of New Jersey. Father Geoffrey M. Colan performed the ceremony at the Roman Catholic Church of the Nativity in Hoboken, N.J.
>
> Dr. Cox, 32, is keeping her name. She is a plastic surgeon and is on the staff of Franklin Hospital in Philadelphia. Mr. Wakesfield, 38, is an attorney in Washington.

VOCABULARY PREVIEW

Read the sentences. Using the context, guess the meanings of the boldfaced words and expressions. Then match them with their definitions. You will hear this vocabulary in the lecture.

1. _____ Since the 1970s there has been a growing **tendency** to address American working women, both single and married, as *Ms.*

2. _____ My daughter's science teacher is **unconventional**. He allows the children to call him by his first name.

3. _____ According to the latest **statistics**, the divorce rate in the United States has increased in the last three years.

4. _____ American women who get married after age thirty are more **likely** to keep their own family names instead of taking their husbands' names.

5. _____ Many **studies** have been done comparing how children and adults learn languages.

6. _____ It is **estimated** that 10 percent of American women do not change their last names when they get married.

7. ____ Young men **tend to** get into more car accidents than young women do.

8. ____ He was elected because of his **reputation** as an honest and hardworking politician.

---

a. the opinion that people have about a person because of what has happened in the past

b. research projects done to find out about a particular subject or problem

c. general change or development in a particular direction; a trend

d. calculated or guessed in a general way (used in reference to the value, size, speed, or amount of something)

e. will probably happen or is probably true

f. collection of numbers that represent facts or measurements

g. often do a particular thing

h. very different from the way people usually behave or think.

PRETEST

1. You are going to hear a lecture in two parts about women's family names in the United States. Listen to the lecture once and take notes (write down the important information). Use your own paper.

2. Use your notes to write short answers to as many of the questions as possible. Work alone. Don't worry if you miss some questions this time. Later you will hear the lecture again.

1. What was the topic of the lecture?

   _____

2. Whose name have most American women traditionally used after marriage?

   _____

3. What important change took place in American society during the 1970s?

   _____

4. How did this change affect women?

   _____

5. In the last thirty years, what has happened to the percentage of women who graduate from college?

   _____

6. What has happened to the percentage of women college graduates who keep their own names after marriage? Why?

   _____

7. According to the lecturer, what will probably happen in the future?

   _____

B. Listening and Note-Taking

LECTURE FORM: THREE FEATURES OF GOOD NOTES

1 Read the information about the form of lecture notes.

Good lecture notes have three features.

1. **Abbreviations and symbols:** To save time and space, use shortened forms (abbreviations) and symbols when you take notes. For example, the symbol ♀ in the model notes that follow means "women," and the abbreviation "soc" means "society." (See Appendix 1 on page 208 for a list of common abbreviations and symbols.)

2. **Key words:** Because lecturers speak quickly, you cannot write every word they say. You should write only the important words. It is not necessary to write complete sentences; include only the words that provide important information.

3. **Indentation:** Indent, or move to the right, to show the difference between main ideas and details. It is common practice to indent information as it becomes more specific. In the model notes you can see three "levels" of notes. The main ideas are on the far left, next to the margin.

2 Study the following model notes for Part 1 of the lecture you heard. Notice the use of indentation, key words, and abbreviations and symbols.

　　　I. Topic: U.S. ♀ don't change fam. name when they get married

○　—new trend

　　　　　Some countries = normal (e.g., Saudi Arabia, Korea)

　　　　　U.S. tradition = married ♀ use husband's last name

　　　II. Changes in U.S. soc. in past 30 yrs

　　　　　1. Soc. more open to untrad. lifestyle → more ♀ go to

　　　　　　college & have career

　　　　　2. Stats:

　　　　　　1970: 8.2% grad. college

　　　　　　1980: 13.6%

　　　　　　1990: 18.4%

○　　　　　2000: 23.6%

---

3 Listen to Part 1 of the lecture again. Follow the model notes as you listen.

LECTURE LANGUAGE: STATISTICAL EXPRESSIONS

Lecturers often use numbers and statistics to support their main points. It is helpful to use symbols or abbreviations to note these statistics and how they support the main points of a lecture.

4 The following statistical expressions are used in the lecture. Write a note-taking symbol or abbreviation for each one. Then work with a classmate and compare answers.

Expression	Symbol or Abbreviation
Percent, percentage	%
number	
less than (1 percent), more than (10 percent)	
to jump / increase / rise	
between (35) and (50) percent	
(it is) estimated	

🎧 **5** Listen to sentences with statistics and write them with key words, abbreviations, and symbols. You will hear each sentence twice.

Example:

You hear: In 1970, only 8.2 percent of American women graduated from college.

You write: 1970: 8.2% of ♀ grad. from college

1. _____

2. _____

3. _____

4. _____

5. _____

🎧 **6** Work with a partner. Exchange notes. Practice restating the sentences you heard using your partner's notes.

TAKING NOTES

🎧 **7** Listen to Part 2 of the lecture again. Take notes on your own paper. Then use your notes to complete the outline below. Use the margin notes to help you.

trend		III. Relationship between ♀ ed. & name change
statistics	○	
		•
		• 1980:
		•
		•
why	○	IV.
		1. ed. ♀ marry later
		2.
		3.
conclusion		V.
	○	

8 Compare these notes with your Pretest notes. What did you do differently this time?

REVIEWING THE LECTURE

9 With one or more classmates, go over the Pretest questions again. Use your notes to discuss the answers.

C. Real Talk: Use What You've Learned

VOCABULARY REVIEW: DISCUSSION

1 Work in small groups. Discuss the following questions. Remember to use the boldfaced expressions from Part One

1. **It's estimated** that about 10 percent of U.S. married women keep their maiden names. Can you estimate the percentage in your country or community?

2. According to **studies**, a small percentage of couples combine their last names with a hyphen when they get married, for example, Mary Cox-Hoffman. What do you think of this custom?

3. Do you think you are **likely** to change your name at some point in your life? Why?

4. These days, many U.S. parents **tend to** give their children **unconventional** names. Is there a similar **tendency** in the place you are from? Give examples.

5. Agree or disagree with the following quotation: "A good **reputation** is better than riches." Explain your opinion.

6. What is your college major? Are **statistics** important in this field?

PRACTICE WITH STATISTICS

2 Work with a partner. Student A, cover the *bottom* chart below and look at the top chart. Student B, cover the *top* chart below and look at the bottom chart. Take turns asking your partner questions about the information that is missing from your box.

Example:

B: What percentage of PhD's did women earn in 1970?

A: Women earned 13.5 percent of PhD's in 1970.

Student A
Percentage of PhD's Earned by Women in the United States, by Year
1970: 13.5
1980: _____
1990: 36.3
2000: _____

Student B
Percentage of PhD's Earned By Women in the United States, by Year
1970: _____
1980: 30.3
1990: _____
2000: 44

3 Compare answers. Then discuss the following question.

What happened to the percentage of women PhD's in the United States between 1970 and 2000?

CHAPTER 2

Let's Get Away!

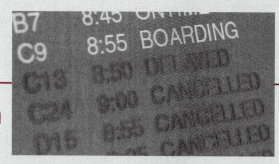

Part One: In Person

A. Prelistening

DISCUSSION

You will hear several people talking about travel. Before you listen, discuss the following questions with a partner or in a small group.

- Where are the people in the pictures?
- What travel problems are they having?
- Have you ever experienced any of these situations?

VOCABULARY PREVIEW

Read the sentences. Using the context, guess the meanings of the boldfaced words and expressions. Then match them with their definitions. You will hear this vocabulary in the recording.

1. _____ Prices at the airport are very high. If you buy anything there, you will probably **pay through the nose**.

2. _____ After paying $300 for a leather jacket, I felt really **ripped off** when I saw the same one in another shop for $220.

3. _____ Jane can put everything she needs for a weekend trip in her **carry-on luggage**.

4. _____ Many professional musicians never **check** their instruments **through** when they travel by plane. They buy a seat for them!

5. _____ We're going on vacation tomorrow, so I'd better **pack** my suitcase tonight.

6. _____ If you want to get a good seat for a popular movie, you need to **show up** early.

7. _____ On schooldays the Smith family's morning **routine** is always the same, but on weekends they don't have to follow a strict schedule.

8. _____ Students were chosen **at random** to give their reports in front of the class.

9. _____ I didn't pack carefully, so when I arrived at my hotel I found my clothes all wrinkled and **messed up**.

10. _____ When his flight was canceled, the traveler **ended up** spending the night in a hotel by the airport.

---

a. schedule or usual way of doing things

b. put things in a bag, box, luggage, and so on

c. not neat; disorderly; spoiled or ruined

d. cheated

e. small suitcase that you can take onto an airplane with you

f. give your suitcases to the airline before your flight and pick them up at the baggage area at the end of your flight

g. arrive or appear

h. find oneself in an unplanned or unexpected situation

i. in no special order

j. pay too much

B. Listening

MAIN IDEAS

🎧 **1** Listen to four people talking about their pet peeves related to travel. (You will easily guess the meaning of *pet peeves* from the context.) Listen and fill in the missing information. Then share your answers with a partner.

Speaker	Pet Peeve
Speaker 1	
Speaker 2	
Speaker 3	
Speaker 4	

DETAILS AND INFERENCES

🎧 **2** Listen again. Which statements are true about the speakers? Mark the statements *T* (true), *F* (false), or *I* (*impossible to know*). Then compare answers with a partner.

SPEAKER 1

_____ 1. works for a tour company

_____ 2. dislikes traveling alone

SPEAKER 2

_____ 3. has traveled outside the United States

_____ 4. dislikes changing money at hotels

SPEAKER 3

_____ 5. takes lots of short vacations

_____ 6. prefers carry-on luggage

_____ 7. can't find scissors in Puerto Rico

_____ 8. has many pairs of scissors

SPEAKER 4

_____ 9. always packs carefully

_____ 10. always travels by plane

LISTENING FOR LANGUAGE

3 Read the information about linking.

FOCUS ON SOUND
Linking

Spoken English can be difficult to understand because speakers don't always pause between words. Instead, they often join words or phrases and pronounce them like one word. In other words, they **link** a word that ends in a consonant sound to a word that begins with a vowel sound. For example:

- *drop off* sounds like *dro poff*
- *in an office* sounds like *i na noffice.*

4 *Listen and repeat the following phrases from the audio. In each phrase, draw a line to connect the linked words.*

Example: it's all folded.

1. can't stand about traveling
2. a group of people
3. part of the day
4. in a hurry
5. travel overseas
6. find an ATM
7. when I travel
8. spend a lot of time
9. take out everything
10. it's impossible

5 *Read the sentences and draw lines to connect linked words. Then listen to the audio to check your answers.*

Example: If I'm in a hurry, I hate it when my bus is late.

1. I end up feeling really ripped off and . . . well, irritated.
2. It is impossible for me to carry my scissors.
3. You get picked out of line for one of the random searches.
4. They take out everything that you spent so much time putting in place so carefully.
5. Everything is all wrinkled and messed up.

6 There are many ways to express irritation or annoyance in English. Study the chart below. (An asterisk * indicates an informal expression.)

CONVERSATION TOOLS
Expressing Annoyance

	Pattern 1	Pattern 2
____ irritates me ____ annoys me ____ bothers me ____ bugs me*	Rude taxi drivers **irritate (annoy, bother, etc.) me.**	It **irritates (bothers, bugs, etc.) me** when the taxi driver is rude.
____ drives me crazy* ____ drives me up the wall* __3__ ticks me off*	Dirty hotel rooms **drive me crazy (tick me off, etc.)**	It **drives me crazy (drives me up a wall)** when my hotel room is dirty.
__1__ can't stand __4__ hate	She **can't stand (hates)** waiting in line.	She **can't stand (hates)** it when she has to wait in line.
____ is annoying __2__ is irritating ____ is frustrating	Lost luggage **is annoying (irritating, etc.).**	It's **annoying (frustrating)** when you lose your luggage.
____ feel annoyed ____ feel irritated ____ feel frustrated		I **feel annoyed** when my train is late.

drove

7 Listen to the recording from Exercise 1 again. If you hear one of the expressions in the chart in Exercise 6, write the number of the speaker who used it next to the expression. The first one is done for you. Then, after listening, work with a partner and compare answers.

8 Work in small groups. Discuss the following questions. Use expressions of annoyance from the chart in Exercise 6.

1. Review the pet peeves from the listening. Which things also bother you?

2. Which pet peeves from the listening are not things that annoy you?

3. What is your biggest pet peeve when you are traveling?

C. Real Talk: Use What You've Learned

VOCABULARY REVIEW: DISCUSSION

Work in small groups. Discuss the following questions. Remember to use the boldfaced expressions from Part One. Focus on linking words and phrases correctly.

1. Have you ever **paid through the nose** for something because you didn't have any other choice?

2. How can a tourist in your country avoid getting **ripped off**?

3. The last time you flew, did you check your bags through, or did you travel with **carry-on luggage**? Why?

4. How long before departure time do you like to **show up** at the airport or station? Why?

5. Where might security officials search people or their bags **at random**? Have you ever had this experience?

6. Have you ever missed a plane, bus, or train? What did you **end up** doing?

7. Describe your packing **routine** before a big trip. What do you do first, second, third, and last, for example?

8. Has your vacation ever been **messed up** by illness, accident, or bad luck?

INTERVIEW

1 Ask three people who are not in your class about their travel pet peeves. If possible, talk to English-speakers. Take notes.

	Person	Pet Peeve
1.		
2.		
3.		

2. In class, take turns sharing the results of your interviews. Make a list on the board of all the pet peeves that you and your classmates heard about.

3. Take a class survey. Have each student vote for his or her biggest pet peeve among those listed on the board. Rank-order the top five pet peeves in your class.

Part Two: On the Phone

A. Prelistening

DISCUSSION

You will hear a customer speaking to a travel agent about buying an airplane ticket. What kind of information will they probably talk about? With a partner, think of two questions the travel agent might ask and two questions the customer might ask.

CUSTOMER

1. _____

2. _____

AGENT

1. _____

2. _____

VOCABULARY PREVIEW

Read the sentences. Using the context, guess the meanings of the boldfaced words and expressions. Then match them with their definitions. You will hear this vocabulary in the phone conversation.

1. _____ Don't forget to pay the **fare** when you get on the bus.

2. _____ Hotel **rates** are more expensive during the holiday season.

3. _____ The train **departs** at 10:00 A.M. and arrives at 1:00 P.M.

4. _____ You should **book** your tickets several weeks before you travel.

5. _____ Most people **purchase** their tickets with a credit card instead of cash.

6. _____ I changed my mind about my trip, but I couldn't get my money back because the ticket was **nonrefundable**.

7. _____ Jenny **stayed over** at her friend's house because she was too tired to drive home.

8. _____ The **deadline** for purchasing the ticket is next Monday.

9. _____ I want to take the train to Disneyland and come back to my hotel the same evening, so I need a **round-trip** ticket.

_____

a. leaves

b. reserve

c. the fee for using transportation

d. time or date when something must be done by

e. prices (per minute, hour, night, etc.)

f. buy

g. taking you to a place and back again

h. not something you can get money back for

i. spent one night

B. Listening

MAIN IDEAS

1 Listen to the conversation. Mark the statements *T* (true) or *F* (false). Then work with a partner and compare answers.

_____ 1. The woman wants to fly to Los Angeles.

_____ 2. The woman wants to buy a round-trip ticket.

_____ 3. The ticket is cheaper if she stays over Saturday night.

_____ 4. The woman has to buy her ticket within forty-eight hours.

_____ 5. The agent reserved a ticket for the woman.

DETAILS AND INFERENCES

🎧 ② Listen again. Fill in the missing information on the ticket below. Then work with a partner and compare answers.

FOR: DOMANICK   JOANNE
ADDRESS: 10920 WILSHIRE BLVD.
PHONE: 555-1212
FAX: 555-3213
AIR TRANSPORTATION: $ _37937_

DEPART FROM	DATE	AIRLINE	TIME	ARRIVE IN
LA	Sept 8	United	11:05	NY

RETURN TRIP

NY	Sept 13	United	4:15	LA

EQUIPMENT: BOEING 767   AIR MILES: 4950 miles round trip
CLASS: COACH   AGENT: MARK

LISTENING FOR LANGUAGE

🎧 ③ Review the information about linking on page 31. Then listen to some sentences from the recording and write the missing words. Listen again and repeat the sentences. Do not pause between linked words. You will hear each sentence twice.

1. If you don't <u>stay over</u> Saturday night, you're ___looking at___ $1,623.68.

2. I ___could if it___ saves money.

3. There's a $75 fee ___for any___ changes once the ___tickets are issued___

4. So I'd have to ___purchase it___ in twenty- ___four hours___.

5. I ___got a um___ 12 noon or 4:15 departure.

6. Can you ___hang on a___ second?

C. Real Talk: Use What You've Learned

VOCABULARY REVIEW: DISCUSSION

Work with a partner or a small group. Discuss the questions. Remember to use the Part Two vocabulary from the box below.

book	fare	rate
deadline	nonrefundable	round-trip
depart	purchase	stay over

1. Where did you go on your latest trip?
2. How much was the fare?
3. How long before departure time did you board?
4. Who booked your ticket: you, a travel agent, or someone else?
5. Did you buy a one-way or round-trip ticket?
6. How did you purchase it: cash, check, or charge?
7. Did you save money by buying a nonrefundable ticket?
8. Did you travel directly to your destination or did you stay over one night in another city?

PROBLEM SOLVING

Discuss the following situations in pairs or groups. Choose a solution and explain your reasons. Share your decision with the whole class.

Situation 1: Your boss asks you to go on a business trip. The company will pay for everything, but you need to make the flight and hotel reservations yourself. Of course, your boss expects you to find the cheapest airfare. You would like to fly on your favorite airline because you can receive thousands of free bonus miles. However, their fares aren't the cheapest.

You will

    a. use your airline and not tell your boss about cheaper fares.

    b. use the cheapest airline to save the company money.

    c. use your airline but pay back the company the price difference.

    d. other: _____

Situation 2: Your boss is sending you on a business trip. You would like to take a family member with you. Your family member could share the hotel room with you and would only have to pay for airfare. It wouldn't cost the company, but your boss probably wouldn't like the idea.

You will

    a. take your relative without telling your boss.

    b. take your relative but tell your boss that he or she joined you as a surprise.

    c. forget about taking your relative.

    d. other: _____

Situation 3: You are standing in line to board an airplane. You have already gone through a security check. You notice that the passenger in front of you is acting strangely. She seems nervous, is holding something under her jacket, and is talking to herself in a way that you don't understand.

You will

    a. report her to a security guard.

    b. speak to her and ask if she is all right.

    c. forget about it and hope she will calm down once she boards the plane.

    d. other: _____

Part Three: On the Air

A. Prelistening

DISCUSSION

You are going to hear several short segments from a radio program called *The Savvy Traveler*. *Savvy* means "clever" or "smart." Before you listen, discuss the following questions with a partner or in a small group.

> ## The Travel Times Newsletter
>
>
>
> • How to avoid airline delays
>
> • Best cross-continental train trips
>
> • Weather information—all continents, all seasons

• What do you think this radio program is probably about?

• Would you want to listen to this type of radio program? Why?

• Have you ever gotten travel information from a radio program?

VOCABULARY PREVIEW

Read the sentences. Using the context, guess the meanings of the boldfaced words and expressions. Then match them with their definitions. You will hear this vocabulary in the radio program.

1. _____ Since September 11, 2001, governments have published new **guidelines** regarding items that travelers can carry on airplanes.

2. _____ Because of better education, the number of AIDS **casualties** is going down in most countries.

3. _____ If you use **insect repellant** on your skin, mosquitoes will not bite you.

4. _____ There was an **outbreak** of food poisoning in the university dormitory after students ate bad meat.

5. _____ **Dusk** is the most dangerous time to drive because it's hard to see when the sun is going down.

6. _____ Smoking can **lead to** cancer and other terrible diseases.

7. _____ Because of poor **visibility** during the storm, airplanes could not land in Chicago.

8. _____ Playing with matches is **hazardous**.

9. _____ Whenever I travel, I make hotel reservations **ahead of time** so that I can be sure to get a good room.

10. _____ Because of a serious **lack of** housing in many large cities, several families have to live together.

_____

a. people who die in a war, by accident, or from disease

b. the ability to see

c. rules

d. before an event happens

e. cause

f. sudden appearance or start of war, fighting, or disease

g. a cream, spray, or lotion to prevent insect bites

h. dangerous

i. not enough of something; a shortage

j. late afternoon or early evening

B. Listening

MAIN IDEAS

1 Read the information about news stories.

> ### THE FIVE W's
>
> News stories are usually short and direct. Typically, the essential information is found at the beginning in the form of the "Five W's": *Who, What, Where, When,* and *Why.* In other words:
>
> - *Who* (or *What*) is the story about?
> - *What* happened?
> - *Where* did it happen?
>
> - *When* did it happen?
> - *Why* did it happen?

2 Listen to four news segments. Fill in the chart. Where a piece of information is not given, put an X in the box. The first item is done for you as an example. Then work with your classmates and compare answers.

Who/What is the story about?	What happened?	Where did it happen?	When did it happen?	Why did it happen?
1. 100 mountain climbers	died in accidents	the Alps	since the end of June	X
2.				
3.				
4.				

DETAILS AND INFERENCES

3 Listen again. Mark the statements *T* (true) or *F* (false).

SEGMENT 1

_____ 1. Government officials warned climbers not to climb alone.

_____ 2. There were more casualties this year than last year.

SEGMENT 2

_____ 3. Eleven people died in the outbreak in 1990.

_____ 4. Mosquitoes are most active at night.

SEGMENT 3

_____ 5. Two hundred people died in an airline crash in Indonesia.

_____ 6. Because of bad visibility, airports were closed in Malaysia.

_____ 7. The State Department warned of hazardous air pollution levels in the United States.

SEGMENT 4

_____ 8. 16,000 people were expected to attend the Olympic Games in Nagano.

_____ 9. In Tokyo it isn't necessary to reserve a hotel room ahead of time.

LISTENING FOR LANGUAGE

4 Study the expressions in the chart for giving advice.

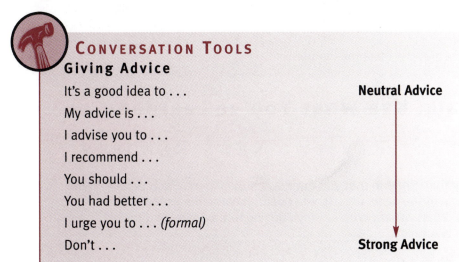

CONVERSATION TOOLS

Giving Advice

It's a good idea to . . .	**Neutral Advice**
My advice is . . .	
I advise you to . . .	
I recommend . . .	
You should . . .	
You had better . . .	
I urge you to . . . _(formal)_	
Don't . . .	**Strong Advice**

🎧 ⑤ Listen to sentences from the radio reports giving advice to travelers. Fill in the missing words.

1. Officials _____ groups _____
   along professional guides rather than reaching for glory by themselves.

2. _____ and _____ insect
   repellent if you're in Florida—that's the _____ of state
   health officials, who warned this week of the possibility of an outbreak of deadly
   encephalitis.

3. Health officials _____ covered—or even indoors—
   from dusk to dawn, when mosquitoes are most active.

4. Singapore radio _____ the elderly and people with
   respiratory problems _____ indoors.

5. If you need to stay overnight in or around Tokyo, _____
   ahead.

⑥ Work in groups. Restate each item in Exercise 5 in three different ways. Try to use all the expressions for giving advice in the chart in Exercise 4.

Example:
Groups *should* take along professional guides.

C. Real Talk: Use What You've Learned

VOCABULARY REVIEW: NEWS REPORTS

Work in groups of four. Pretend that you are news announcers. Each person in the group will retell one of the news reports you heard. Include the essential information (Who, What, When, Where, Why), advice to travelers, and the vocabulary in the box below.

News Report 1	News Report 2	News Report 3	News Report 4
casualties	dusk	hazardous	ahead
guidelines	insect repellant	lead to	lack of
	outbreak	visibility	

ROLE PLAY

Work with a partner. Student A is an American who wants to visit Student B's country. Student A asks for advice about one of the topics below. Role play the conversation. Afterward, switch roles and speak about another topic. Try to use expressions for giving advice. Also, pay attention to stressed words and linking.

TOPICS

- visa requirements
- food and water
- insects and animals to beware of
- traffic laws, problems, or restrictions
- crime
- seasons to avoid
- dangerous areas or places
- equipment or clothes to take
- money, banking

Example:

Student A: Hey, Ahmet, my boss just told me I have to go to Istanbul for a big conference. It's going to be in the second week of January. How's the weather at that time of year? What kind of clothes should I take?

Student B: It's very cold and windy in Istanbul in January. Sometimes it even snows, so you should take a warm coat and gloves.

Part Four: In Class

A. Prelistening

DISCUSSION

You will hear a lecture about the fear of flying. Before you listen, discuss the following questions with a partner or in a small group.

- Look at the picture. Compare the two passengers. How are they feeling? What might the person near the window be worried about?

- Are you or is someone you know afraid of flying?

- What can a person do to overcome a fear of flying?

VOCABULARY PREVIEW

Read the sentences. Using the context, guess the meanings of the boldfaced words and expressions. Then match them with their definitions. You will hear this vocabulary in the lecture.

1. _____ Tom felt **intense** pain when he broke his arm.

2. _____ Tammy is very afraid of spiders even though she knows her fear is **irrational**.

3 _____ Tom began **therapy** with a psychologist in order to overcome his shyness.

4. _____ During the earthquake, people became **panic-stricken** and ran into the street without thinking about what they were doing.

5. _____ As the soldiers waited for the battle to start, their impatience and **anxiety** rose.

6. _____ The most important **phase** of my education was the time I spent in high school.

7. _____ Don't **confront** a car thief by yourself; just call the police.

8. _____ The child couldn't participate in sports because of his heart **disorder**.

9. _____ A headache and a cough are **symptoms** of a cold.

10. _____ The mother's soft and kind voice helped **eliminate** all the child's fears.

---

a. professional treatment of an illness or problem

b. a step or stage in a process

c. strong (feeling or emotion)

d. nervous fear about a future event

e. face a difficulty or danger directly

f. sickness (of the mind or body)

g. remove or get rid of something you don't want

h. very afraid; unable to control fear

i. without reason or logic

j. a sign that a problem exists

B. Listening and Note-Taking

LECTURE ORGANIZATION: INTRODUCTIONS

1 Read the information about introductions.

> When listening to lectures, pay special attention to the introduction. It can help you to do the following:
>
> - Anticipate the main points.
> - Predict the organization of the lecture.
> - Plan your lecture notes.
>
> Listen for sentences that state the goal(s) or give an overview of the lecture.
>
> For example:
>
> Today, we're going to focus on _____ and _____.
>
> The main purpose of my presentation is to _____.
>
> We're not going to cover _____; the focus will be on _____.

🎧 ② **Listen to the lecture introduction. Based on the information, which topics do you expect to hear about in the lecture? Write _Y_ (yes), _N_ (no), or _M_ (maybe).**

_____ 1. What *phobia* means

_____ 2. One common phobia

_____ 3. Why people are afraid to fly

_____ 4. How friends can help people with this problem

_____ 5. How professionals can cure this problem

_____ 6. Symptoms of the problem

LECTURE LANGUAGE: DEFINING TERMS

③ **Read the information about ways of defining terms.**

When a lecturer defines a term, it is important to take notes. Although you may think you already know the term, the lecturer may define it differently. On an exam, you will probably be asked about the exact definition given in the lecture.

Here are some expressions for defining terms:

Let me give you *the definition of* a phobia.

A phobia can *be defined as* . . .

Let me *define* that.

Phobia means . . .

Phobia refers to . . .

By phobia, I *mean* . . .

4 Listen to several definitions. Write each term and take notes on its definition.

Example:

You hear: One definition of *therapy* is the treatment of an illness over a long period of time, without the use of medicine.

You write: therapy = treatment of illness, over long time, w/o medicine

Term	Definition
1.	
2.	
3.	
4.	

TAKING NOTES

5 Listen to the lecture. Take notes on your own paper. Then look at the outline on page 48. It includes the main ideas and some details from the lecture. Use your notes to complete the outline. Refer to Harry's list on page 49 as necessary. Use the margin notes to help you.

Remember to do the following:

- Indent.
- Write key words only.
- Abbreviate to save time and space.

introduction

definition of phobia

Phobia:

details / statistics about fear of flying

- plane travel = 20 x safer than car travel
-

what can help?

Treatment:

In therapist's office

Phase 1:

Phase 2:

Phase 3:

In the real world (phase 4):

1st day:

conclusion

Harry's List of Feared Situations

Feared Situation	Rating
• Taking a friend to airport and dropping him off outside	1
• Walking into airport terminal	2
• Going through metal detector	2
• Going to the departure gate	3
• Checking in at flight counter	4
• Going to boarding ramp and handing ticket to attendant	5
• Walking down the ramp as far as the entrance to the plane	6
• Walking onto the plane and greeting the attendant	7
• Finding seat	7
• Sitting down and putting on seatbelt	8
• Sitting in plane on the ground	8
• Taxiing to runway	9
• Taking off	10
• Experiencing turbulence in flight	10
• Landing	10

REVIEWING THE LECTURE

6 **Work with one or more classmates. Use notes to discuss the following questions.**

1. How is a phobia different from normal fear?

2. How common is aerophobia?

3. What is desensitization?

4. How many phases does the treatment consist of? Describe each step.

5. In your opinion, why does this treatment work so well?

C. Real Talk: Use What You've Learned

VOCABULARY REVIEW: DISCUSSION

Work in pairs or small groups. Discuss the following questions. Remember to use the boldfaced words and expressions from Part Four.

1. What situations or things give you **anxiety**? Do you have a good reason to fear these situations, or are your fears **irrational**?

2. Do you know anyone who suffers (or has suffered in the past) from a phobia? How does it affect his or her life?

3. Although the lecture didn't say, why do you think some people develop such an **intense** fear of some things?

4. Describe the behavior of a **panic-stricken** person a) in a fire; b) during a final exam; c) in a broken elevator.

PROBLEM SOLVING

Work in small groups. Follow these steps.

1. Choose one of the phobias:
   - fear of spiders
   - fear of enclosed places
   - fear of heights
   - fear of crowds
   - fear of dogs
   - fear of the dark

2. Plan a course of treatment for a person who suffers from a phobia.
   - Review the four phases of desensitization therapy you learned from the lecture.
   - Prepare a list of feared situations like Harry's.
   - Discuss how you would help the person face each situation in real life.

3. Present your treatment plan to another small group or the whole class.

CHAPTER 3

Looking for Love

Part One: In Person

A. Prelistening

DISCUSSION

You will hear two people talking about relationships. Before you listen, discuss the following questions with a partner or in a small group.

- In your country or culture, how common is it for young people to marry someone from a different country, ethnic group, or religion?

- How would your family feel if you did this?

VOCABULARY PREVIEW

Read the sentences. Using the context, guess the meanings of the boldfaced words and expressions. Then match them with their definitions. You will hear this vocabulary in the conversation.

1. _____ Tom and his girlfriend see each other almost every day, so I think they are **pretty serious**.

2. _____ Nancy cried all night when her boyfriend **broke up with** her.

3. _____ If you study hard, **chances are** you'll do well on the exam.

4. _____ I **feel bad for** people who are old and lonely.

5. _____ When our neighbors argue, we just **stay out of it**.

6. _____ Yuki was accepted by Harvard University **on the basis of** his grades and TOEFL score.

7. _____ **As far as** salaries **go**, New York is one of the best cities to work in.

8. _____ Sharon invited all her classmates to her birthday party because she didn't want anyone to feel sad about being **left out**.

---

a. there is a high probability

b. regarding, concerning

c. because of, thanks to

d. not included

e. don't get involved, don't interfere

f. their relationship is very close

g. have sympathy, be sad about

h. ended the relationship

B. Listening

MAIN IDEAS

Listen to a conversation between Kathy, a young Korean-American woman, and Mark, a young Caucasian ("white") American man. Listen and take notes on the answers to the questions below. Do not write complete sentences. After listening, work with a classmate and compare answers.

1. What question does Mark ask Kathy?

_____

2. What is her answer?

_____

3. What question does Kathy ask Mark?

_____

4. How does Mark answer Kathy's question?

_____

5. Are Kathy's and Mark's attitudes toward marriage similar or different?

_____

DETAILS AND INFERENCES

2 Listen to parts of the conversation again. How does each person below feel about marrying a person of a different nationality or religion? Circle the speaker's attitude and take notes on the speaker's reason, if given. Work with a classmate and compare answers.

Person	Attitude	Reason (if given)
1. Kathy—past	for against no opinion	
2. Kathy's mother	for against no opinion	
3. Kathy's father	for against no opinion	
4. Kathy—now	for against no opinion	
5. Mark	for against no opinion	

LISTENING FOR LANGUAGE

3 Read the information about reductions.

FOCUS ON SOUND
Reductions

In natural spoken English there are many *reductions* or *reduced forms*. These are words and phrases that are not pronounced the way they are written. Instead, their pronunciation changes in one or more of the following ways, causing the word(s) to be shorter.

- Some vowels and consonants may disappear or change. For example:

  want to ➤ *wanna*
  should have ➤ *shoulda*
  don't know ➤ *dunno*

- Syllables may disappear. For example:

  going to ➤ *gonna*
  do you ➤ *d'ya*

Reduced forms are usually unstressed words such as auxiliary verbs (*do, be, have*), articles (*a, the*), pronouns (*he, they*), and prepositions (*to, for*).

Because reduced forms are normally unstressed, they can be hard to hear and understand in real conversation.

4 Listen to these examples from the conversation; notice the changes in vowels, consonants, and syllables.

You read	You hear
a. How do you think your parents would feel if you married someone who wasn't Korean?	a. How *d'ya* think *yer* parents '*d* feel if *ya* married someone who wasn't Korean?
b. I'm probably going to meet someone who's not Korean.	b. I'm *probly gonna* meet someone who's not Korean.
c. My dad just kind of stays out of it.	c. My dad just *kinda* stays out of it.
d. It would be beneficial if he was Korean and spoke Korean.	d. It would be beneficial if he was Korean '*n*' spoke Korean.

5 Close your book. Listen to the examples in Exercise 4 again. Repeat each sentence without reading it. Focus on pronouncing the stressed and reduced forms correctly.

6 Listen to sentences with stressed words, reduced forms, and linking. After each sentence, pause the recording. Then write each sentence.

1. _____

2. _____

3. _____

4. _____

5. _____

C. Real Talk: Use What You've Learned

VOCABULARY REVIEW: DISCUSSION

1 Read the statements below. Are they true for you? Write *Yes, No*, or *Maybe* in the blanks. Then discuss your answers with your classmates. Remember to use the vocabulary from Part One.

_____ 1. I have **broken up with** someone because my parents did not like him or her, even though we were **pretty serious**.

_____ 2. **Chances are** I will marry someone who has the same religion as I do.

_____ 3. I **feel bad for** hurt or homeless animals.

_____ 4. I will choose my husband or wife **on the basis of** how much money he or she makes.

_____ 5. **As far as** education **goes**, I don't care if my husband or wife has more or less than I do.

_____ 6. I often felt **left out** as a child.

_____ 7. If two of my close friends had an argument, I would **stay out of it**.

2 Read about the following situation. Then discuss the question that follows. Look for places where you can use reduced forms such as *gonna, wanna, shoulda*, etc.

Situation: While studying in the United States, you met an American and started going out with him or her. After a few months you began to get serious about each other, and now you have started to talk about the possibility of marriage. Your boyfriend or girlfriend is willing to learn your language and live in your country. The problem is that you know your parents will be very angry and hurt if you marry an American.

Question: What do you think you would do in this situation? Complete the following sentence, and explain your reasons.

Chances are I would

    a. break up with him or her.

    b. get married, live in my country, and hope that my parents will accept it someday.

    c. get married and live in the United States.

    d. live together in the United States without getting married.

    e. other: _____

Part Two: On the Phone

A. Prelistening

DISCUSSION

You will hear a phone conversation about one way to find a mate. Before you listen, discuss the following questions with a partner or in a small group.

Read this list of ways to find a mate. Which ones are you familiar with? Which ones have you used?

- newspaper "personal ads"
- Internet dating sites
- matchmaking services
- personal introductions by family or friends
- "singles" bars or dances
- (other)

VOCABULARY PREVIEW

Read the sentences. Using the context, guess the meanings of the boldfaced words and expressions. Then match them with their definitions. You will hear this vocabulary in the conversation.

1. _____ My English teacher is a single woman. I would love to **match** her **up** with my uncle. I think they would make a great couple!

2. _____ After her divorce, Dianne discovered that the **pool** of single men her age was very small.

3. _____ The matchmaker created a written **profile**, containing personal information and her private notes on each of her clients.

4. _____ Linda and Craig went out a few times, but they stopped dating because there was no **chemistry** between them.

5. _____ My grandmother has nineteen grandchildren. Each year she sends a birthday gift to **every single one** of them.

6. _____ Two hundred people applied for a job. The company **screened** all of them. Then it chose ten people to be interviewed.

7. _____ Telephone salespeople know they have fifteen seconds or less to **hook** new customers. That is why they talk so fast.

8. _____ A: I want to rent an apartment near the university. Can you give me a **ballpark figure** of what it will cost?

   B: For a small one-bedroom, I'd say you'll need to pay between $800 and $1,000 a month.

9. _____ When you eat in a restaurant, **keep in mind** that you need to give the waiter a 15 percent tip.

---

a. all; each; every one

b. physical or sexual attraction

c. approximate cost

d. arrange for two people to meet

e. remember

f. description of a person; biography

g. aggressively try to persuade someone to join an organization or buy a product

h. checked the backgrounds or qualifications before meeting face to face

i. group of people available for a certain purpose or task

B. Listening

MAIN IDEAS

🎧 ① Listen to Jay, a single man, making a phone call to a company called Bright Futures. Fill in the chart as you listen. Write *No Info* if an item is not mentioned.

Information about	
Jay	**Bright Futures**
Reason for call:	Type of service:
Referred by:	History of company:
Age:	Size:
Occupation:	How it works:
Final decision:	Cost:

② Now work with a classmate and compare answers.

DETAILS AND INFERENCES

🎧 ③ Listen to the phone call again and answer the questions.

1. Bright Futures

    a. is a matchmaking service.

    b. is a private membership club.

    c. is an Internet dating service.

2. To help members find people to date, Bright Futures uses

    a. a website.

    b. videotapes.

    c. computers.

3. According to Linda, you have to be careful with Internet dating sites because

    a. people may lie about themselves.

    b. some sites take your money.

    c. everyone will want to screen you.

4. What is the first thing Jay must do if he decides to join Bright Futures?

    a. pay the fee

    b. send in his profile

    c. go to the company's office

4 Look at the list of adjectives below. Choose three that describe Linda and three that describe Jay. Write them in the chart. Then work with a partner and explain your answers.

aggressive	enthusiastic	polite
confident	funny	rich
embarrassed	hesitant	shy
energetic	lonely	

Adjectives to Describe Jay	Adjectives to Describe Linda
1.	1.
2.	2.
3.	3.

LISTENING FOR LANGUAGE

5 Read the information about ways to interrupt politely in English.

CONVERSATION TOOLS
Interrupting

In many cultures it is considered rude or disrespectful to interrupt a person who is speaking. English speakers, in contrast, interrupt each other frequently, especially in informal situations. The following words and phrases are commonly used:

I don't mean to interrupt, (but)   more formal
Excuse me for interrupting, (but)
Pardon me, (but)
May I say something here?
Can I just jump in here?   less formal
Wait a minute.
Hold on a second.
Sorry for butting in, (but)
Yeah, but . . .   informal

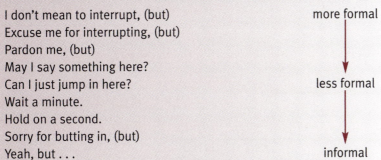

🎧 ⑥ Listen to two segments from the conversation again. Write the expressions Jay uses to interrupt Linda.

1. _____

2. _____

⑦ Read the information about stressing words for emphasis.

FOCUS ON SOUND
Stressing Words for Emphasis

In Chapter 1 you learned the basic stress pattern of English sentences. You learned that normally content words are stressed but function words are not. This is not a strict rule, however. In fact, speakers can stress any words they choose in order to emphasize them. For example:

Basic pattern: What we do is we let you choose.

With emphasis: What we do is we let **you** choose.

🎧 ⑧ Listen to sentences from the conversation. Underline the words that are stressed for emphasis.

Example: We're <u>not</u> a matchmaking service.

1. What we do is we let you choose.

2. Let me answer these other points that I hadn't gotten to before.

3. One, and probably first and foremost, is the fact that we prescreen everybody who walks through here.

4. We screen you as well as you screening us.

5. But do keep in mind that the best way to get the most information is to see us in person.

C. Real Talk: Use What You've Learned

VOCABULARY REVIEW: CONVERSATION

Work with a partner. Fill in the blanks with Part Two vocabulary from the box below. Then read the conversation.

ballpark figure	hook	pool
chemistry	keep in mind	profile
every single one	match up	screen

Client: How does your dating service work?

Salesman: We are a membership club for busy single people who don't have a lot of time to date. We have a huge _____ of people to choose from. We

1

meet _____ of our members in person . . .

2

Client: Excuse me for interrupting, but what do you do? You _____

3

people _____?

3 (continued)

Salesman: No, we let you choose. We are like a library. You come in and you choose the people you want to meet.

Client: How do I decide?

Salesman: Well, as I was saying, we _____ each of our members,

4

and we write up a _____ on them. We take their picture and we

5

also make a five- or six-minute video. Then when clients come in, they sit in our library and they look at these materials and choose people they'd like to meet. Then we contact those people and they come in and look at your profile, and if they also feel there might be _____ there, then we give you each other's

6

contact information.

Client: That sounds great. Uh, how much does the membership cost?

Salesman: I'm afraid I can't tell you that over the phone. You have to come into our office. Believe me, you'll be glad you did.

Client: Now you're trying to _____ me. Can you at least give me a

                          7
_____?

       8

Salesman: I'm sorry, I can't. You have to come in. But _____ that

                                                         9
we have over 5,000 members to choose from, and since we started our company, we've been averaging four or five weddings each month.

Client: Let me think about it.

INTERRUPTING GAME

Sit in groups of three or four. Take turns talking about one of the topics below. As one student speaks, the others should interrupt at every opportunity. Use stress to emphasize important words.

Example:

A: A funny thing happened to me last night. I went to a movie . . .

B: Excuse me for interrupting, but who did you go with?

A: My brother. Anyway, we went to a movie . . .

C: Pardon me, but which movie did you see?

A: *Le Divorce.* As I was saying, I went to a movie, and as I was standing in line . . .

TOPICS

- how you met your boyfriend / girlfriend / husband / wife
- the best / worst date you have ever had
- a wedding you attended

Part Three: On the Air

A. Prelistening

PREDICTION

You will hear a radio interview with people who have chosen not to get married. Before you listen, discuss the following questions with a partner or in a small group.

- What are three reasons for staying single?
- What are three reasons to get married?

Stay single

1. _____

2. _____

3. _____

Get married

1. _____

2. _____

3. _____

VOCABULARY PREVIEW

Read the sentences. Using the context, guess the meanings of the boldfaced words and expressions. Then match them with their definitions. You will hear this vocabulary in the interview.

1. _____ Sometimes I enjoy being with other people; at other times I prefer **solitude**.

2. _____ Tom and Lily had a **committed** relationship for four years before they decided to get married.

3. _____ Most of my **thirty-something** friends are already married.

4. _____ Jack and his wife plan to have five children, but I **wonder about** their ability to support them.

5. _____ A happy family and an interesting career make me feel **fulfilled**.

6. _____ In southern California the supply of fresh water is **dwindling**, and each year the state has to import more water.

7. _____ Don't **assume** that Greg is rich just because he drives a BMW.

8. _____ After high school, Angie wants to **pursue** a college degree.

---

a. going down in quantity

b. doubt or question

c. think that something is true, though you have no proof of it

d. try to achieve

e. being alone

f. satisfied

g. between thirty and thirty-nine years old

h. serious, deeply loyal

B. Listening

MAIN IDEAS

🎧 **1** Listen to the radio interview. Complete the notes on the main reasons why the three people prefer to stay single.

	Age	Reasons for Choosing to Stay Single
Neil L.	fifty-two	He likes his: 1. _____ 2. _____ 3. <u>privacy</u> 4. _____
Jennifer S.		She isn't sure whether _____
Terri W.	early fifties	1. She doesn't feel pressure to marry because ____ _____ 2. _____

2 Work with a partner and compare answers. Then review your list of reasons for staying single in the Prelistening activity on page 63. Which of these reasons were also mentioned by the people in the interview?

DETAILS AND INFERENCES

🎧 **3** Listen again. Mark the statements *T* (true) or *F* (false).

_____ 1. Neil has been married for ten years.

_____ 2. Neil is against marriage in general.

_____ 3. Jennifer might get married someday.

_____ 4. Most of Jennifer's friends want to stay single.

_____ 5. Terri never gets lonely.

_____ 6. Terri feels she has a great life.

LISTENING FOR LANGUAGE

④ Read the information about ways of expressing doubt or uncertainty.

CONVERSATION TOOLS
Expressing Doubt or Uncertainty

There are many ways of expressing doubt or uncertainty in English. They include:

Structure	Example
(She) wonders about ⎫ ⎬ + noun (I'm) not sure of ⎭	• She wonders about marriage all the time. • I'm not sure of the answer.
(She) wonders about what, why, how . . .	• She wonders about what to do.
(I'm) not sure ⎫ ⎬ + if / whether + clause (I) don't know ⎬ (I) doubt ⎭	• I'm not sure whether I want to get married or not. • I don't know if I should get married. • I doubt if I will get married.

🎧 ⑤ Listen to part of the interview again. Write the expressions of doubt or uncertainty you hear.

1. _____

2. _____

3. _____

C. Real Talk: Use What You've Learned

VOCABULARY REVIEW: DISCUSSION

Work with a partner or a small group. Discuss the questions on the next page. Remember to use the Part Three vocabulary from the box below.

assume	dwindling	pursue	thirty-something
committed	fulfilled	solitude	wonder about

1. Where do you usually go when you need **solitude**?

2. Do you think it's possible to live a fulfilled life without being in a **committed** relationship?

3. What does your society think of adults who are **thirty-something** and single? What do people **assume** about them?

4. What is your most important goal right now: to **pursue** an education, a career, or marriage?

5. Do you ever **wonder about** your duty to make your parents happy?

EXPRESSING DOUBTS

Lisa and Greg have been dating since they met at a party last year. They are thinking about getting married. Read the information under their pictures. What uncertainties or doubts might they have about each other? Use expressions of doubt or uncertainty to say what Lisa and Greg might be thinking.

LISA

thirty-two years old
pharmacist
earns $75,000 a year
divorced
has one child
plays piano
loves Greg

GREG

thirty-eight years old
artist
earns $30,000 a year
never married
enjoys being single
loves jazz
loves Lisa

GROUP PRESENTATION

Work in groups of four. Follow these steps.

1. With your classmates, brainstorm about the advantages and disadvantages of being single. Make a worksheet like this on your own paper:

Single Men		Single Women	
Advantages	Disadvantages	Advantages	Disadvantages

2. Present your group's ideas to the whole class. Each person in the group should talk about one advantage or disadvantage.

3. As groups take turns presenting, one student should keep a master list of advantages and disadvantages on the board.

4. Take a class vote: Is it easier for men or for women to be single?

Part Four: In Class

A. Prelistening

DISCUSSION

You will hear a lecture about the biology of love. Before you listen, discuss the following questions with a partner or in a small group.

1. Look at the cartoon. What is the couple thinking of? What is their idea of love? How about the scientist?

2. Scientists say there are many kinds of love. What do you think?

3. List five people you love and your relationship with them (for example: husband, child, best friend, uncle, teacher). Discuss how the quality of the love is similar or different in each relationship.

_____

_____

_____

_____

_____

VOCABULARY PREVIEW

Read the sentences. Using the context, guess the meanings of the boldfaced words and expressions. Then match them with their definitions. You will hear this vocabulary in the lecture.

1. _____ Lisa and Alex fell **head over heels in love**. They got married soon after that.

2. _____ **Hormones** cause teenagers' bodies and behavior to change.

3. _____ Do you believe that men have a stronger sex **drive** than women?

4. _____ If you are **responsible for** an accident, you have to pay for fixing the damage.

5. _____ Peter is almost as **passionate** about his girlfriend as he is about football.

6. _____ In many cultures, the color black is **associated with** death.

7. _____ Jason had many girlfriends before he finally decided to **settle down** with Ashley.

8. _____ Although Myra is married and lives far from her parents, she still has a very strong **attachment** to them.

---

a. very eager or excited

b. close connection or relationship

c. find a permanent partner to live with

d. related to; occur together with

e. natural need that must be satisfied

f. deeply and totally in love

g. the cause of an event or action

h. brain chemicals that influence the body's growth, development, and health

B. Listening and Note-Taking

LECTURE ORGANIZATION: TRANSITIONS

1 Read the information about transitions.

Transitions are words and phrases that connect the sections of a lecture (or composition). They serve as signals that the speaker is moving from one point to another. They also make understanding easier by helping listeners to predict what the speaker will say next.

English speakers use many kinds of transitions. For example:

Words	OK, now, so, first, second, next, finally
Phrases	to begin, to continue, in conclusion, for example, on the other hand, in contrast
Sentences	Let's look at a couple of examples. I want to begin by explaining . . . Let's review.
Summaries	We've just looked at . . . , now let's look at . . . We've seen that . . . In summary, . . .

2 Listen to sentences from the lecture and fill in the missing transitions. Then work with a partner and compare answers.

1. So according to Dr. Fisher, the three stages of love are lust, romantic love, and attachment. _____, lust, refers to a very powerful physical or sexual attraction to another person.

2. Now, _____, according to Dr. Fisher, is what she calls romantic love.

3. Recent research has shown that high levels of dopamine are in the brains of people who are in love. _____, scientists at the University of London did a very interesting experiment with a group of volunteers who described themselves as being newly in love.

4. _____ the volunteers were shown pictures of their lovers.

5. When the volunteers saw pictures of their lovers, the part of the brain that makes dopamine, this pleasure hormone, was very active. _____,
when they looked at pictures of their friends, there was no such activity.

6. OK. _____ we come to the third stage of love, what Dr. Fisher calls the attachment phase.

7. So, _____ what we've learned so far about the biology of love.

LECTURE FORM: OUTLINING

3 Read the information in the box.

Some students like to take notes in the form of an *outline*. Outlines use a system of indentations, letters, and numbers to represent the organization of ideas in a lecture (or composition). Look at the following model; notice the indentations. Also, notice that similar letters and numbers are in a straight vertical line. In other words, II is under I; B is under A, etc.

I. Major topic
   A. First division of major topic I
      1. Detail concerning division A
         a. further detail about 1
         b. further detail about 1
      2. Another detail concerning division A
   B. Second division of major topic I
      1. Detail concerning division B
II. Second major topic

If you use an outline to take notes, you don't need to write transitions. You use indentation, letters, and numbers instead of words.

TAKING NOTES

 4 Listen to the lecture. Take notes on your own paper. Then use your notes to complete the outline. Remember, in an outline you do not need to write transitions. Use the margin notes to help you.

introduction	I. Topic:
	Love = bio process
stages	II. Dr. Helen Fisher (Rutgers U.): love →
	3 stages w/ diff. chemicals active in brain
1st stage	A. Lust
definition	1. powerful sexual attract. to another person
hormone	2. hormone = testosterone
	a. not just male hormone
	b.
2nd stage	B. Romantic love
characteristics	1. become emotionally attached
	2.
hormone	3.
research study	4. study @ U. of London
1st step	a.
2nd step	b.
	c. sci. used MRI to record brain activ.
results	5. when vol. saw pic. of lovers →
	when pic. of friends →
conclusion	6.

(continued)

3rd stage	C.
characteristics	1.
	2.
hormone	3.
animal research	a.
	b.
humans	c.
role of oxytocin	4.
	III.
conclusion	

REVIEWING THE LECTURE

⑤ **Work with one or more classmates. Use your notes to discuss the following questions.**

1. Describe the three stages of love, according to Dr. Helen Fisher. For each stage, explain:
   • which hormone is active in the brain.
   • how people feel and behave.
2. Describe the University of London study.
3. What kind of process is love, according to scientists?

C. Real Talk: Use What You've Learned

VOCABULARY REVIEW: DISCUSSION

Work in pairs or in small groups. Discuss the following questions. Remember to use the boldfaced expressions from Part Four.

1. Have you ever been **head over heels in love**?

2. What is a good age to **settle down**, in your opinion? Is it different for men and women?

3. Do you think **passionate** love is necessary in a marriage?

4. In your opinion, which invention is most **responsible for** improving the quality of people's lives in the last fifty years?

5. In some countries, food animals are given **hormones** to make them grow faster and larger. Do you think this is safe?

6. In your culture or community, which colors are **associated with** the following life events:
   - the birth of a boy or girl
   - death
   - marriage
   - holidays (For example, in the United States people wear red, white, and blue for the Fourth of July.)

7. How are people's lives affected if they do not have a close **attachment** to their parents early in life?

8. After hearing the lecture, which statement do you agree with more:
   - Love is a romantic feeling.
   - Love is a biological **drive**.

EXPANSION: LOVE IDIOMS

Work alone, in pairs, or in small groups.

1 Below is a list of idioms associated with love, in addition to the two that the lecturer used. Your teacher will assign you or your group one or more idioms to define.

be/get turned on	love at first sight
(be) madly in love	make a commitment
fall head over heels in love	puppy love
go steady	settle down
have a crush on somebody	sweep someone off his/her feet
have an affair	tie the knot

2 Out of class, ask an English speaker to define your idiom(s), or use a dictionary. Prepare to report the idiom and the definition to the whole class.

3 As you listen to your classmates explain the idioms and their definitions, place each one in the appropriate column. Compare and discuss your answers.

Lust	Romantic Love	Attachment
Be/Get turned on	Fall head over heels in love	Settle down

4 In groups, use the idioms to ask and answer questions about your relationship experience. (*Note*: If someone asks you a question that makes you feel uncomfortable, simply say "Pass.")

SAMPLE QUESTIONS

- How old were you the first time you *had a crush* on somebody?
- Do you believe in *love at first sight*?
- What is a good age for men and women to *tie the knot*?

CHAPTER 4

Music to My Ears

Part One: In Person

A. Prelistening

DISCUSSION

You will hear several people talk about their favorite type of music. Before you listen, work in small groups, and list as many different types of music as you can think of. For each type, briefly tell what you know about the origin and characteristics of this music. Then share your list with another group or with the whole class.

Example: reggae
- started on the island of Jamaica
- famous artist: Bob Marley
- uses electric guitars, drums, and some native instruments
- strong rhythm

VOCABULARY PREVIEW

Read the sentences. Using the context, guess the meanings of the boldfaced words and expressions. Then match them with their definitions. You will hear this vocabulary in the short interviews.

1. _____ I like songs with a strong **beat** that I can dance to.

2. _____ The whole crowd was clapping and **tapping** their feet to the music.

3. _____ Norah Jones's voice is very **soothing**. I listen to her when I want to relax.

4. _____ The classical composer Handel wrote religious music for huge **choruses** of 100 voices or more.

5. _____ **Lyrics** are often hard to understand because singers often don't pronounce them clearly.

6. _____ Most of the music I listen to fits into the pop **genre**, but I also enjoy listening to jazz.

7. _____ The singer sang so softly that no one could **make out** which song he was singing.

8. _____ Many modern songs are based on traditional folk **melodies**.

---

a. type, class, or category of music, art, writing, etc.

b. rhythm; regular, repeated pattern of sounds or movements

c. tunes

d. gentle; calming

e. hitting your fingers or foot lightly against something

f. words of a song

g. large group of people who sing together

h. just barely able to hear, see, or understand

B. Listening

MAIN IDEAS

🎧 **1** Listen to several people talking about their favorite type of music and fill in the chart. Then compare your answers with those of your classmates.

Speaker	Favorite type(s) of music	Why he or she likes it
1. Sarah	jazz	- can be fast, slow, soft, loud - different rhythms -
2. Kathleen		
3. Bonnie		
4. Dennis		
5. Andrea		
6. Spencer		

DETAILS AND INFERENCES

🎧 **2** Listen again. Write the name of the speaker who . . .

1. likes listening to acoustic instruments　　　　＿＿＿＿＿＿＿＿＿

2. listens to music while cooking　　　　＿＿＿＿＿＿＿＿＿

3. thinks the human voice is the most wonderful instrument　　　　＿＿＿＿＿＿＿＿＿

4. might be a writer   _____

5. enjoys watching musicians play live music   _____

6. loves orchestras   _____

LISTENING FOR LANGUAGE

3 Read the information about denotation and connotation.

CONVERSATION TOOLS
Denotation and Connotation

Some words that appear to be synonyms are actually not synonymous at all. For example, the words *unusual* and *weird* both mean that something is different or out of the ordinary. However, English speakers use these words differently.

Unusual = different in a *neutral* way   Example: She has an unusual voice.

Weird = different in a *negative* way   Example: Björk has a weird voice. I don't
                                                          really like it.

Unusual and *weird* have the same general meaning, or *denotation*. However, they differ in their *connotation*, that is, their emotional or implied meaning. Words can have positive, negative, or neutral connotations. Moreover, the same word can have different connotations, depending on how a speaker uses it.

4 Study the following sets of adjectives for describing music. Discuss unfamiliar words with your classmates or use a dictionary to look them up.

1. _____ loud   _____ soft   _____ fast   _____ slow

2. _____ subtle   _____ soft   _____ rhythmic   _____ soothing

3. _____ down-to-earth _____ honest   _____ overproduced

4. _____ loud   _____ screaming

5 Listen again to selected sentences from the interviews. Listen for the positive, negative, or neutral connotation of the adjectives in Exercise 4. During the pauses between sentences, write + [positive], – [negative], or 0 [neutral] in the spaces. Hint: Words that appear more than once may have different connotations.

6 Add three more adjectives to the list in Exercise 4 that you can use to talk about music. Share them with a partner. Discuss whether their connotation is positive, negative, or neutral.

C. Real Talk: Use What You've Learned

Vocabulary Review: Discussion

Work in small groups. Discuss the following questions. Remember to use the boldfaced expressions from Part One.

1. When you listen to songs, what is more important to you: the **lyrics** or the **melody**?
2. Do you like to dance? Which music has the best **beat** for dancing, in your opinion?
3. Have you ever attended a concert in which the audience was making so much noise that you couldn't **make out** what the band was singing?
4. Do you like to sing? Have you ever sung in a **chorus**?
5. Most cultures have one or more unique types of music. Tell about one **genre** from your culture. Describe the music and the musicians.
6. Do you listen to music when you are worried or troubled? If so, what kind of music do you find **soothing**?

Oral Presentation

1 Give a one-minute talk in which you answer these questions:

- What is your favorite type of music?
- Why do you like it?

Use at least five adjectives for describing music in your talk. If possible, bring a recording of your favorite music to class and play a short segment of it as an introduction to your talk.

2 Create a chart like the one on page 78. As you listen to your classmates' presentations, take notes. Afterward, work with a partner and compare notes.

Survey

1 Interview three English speakers about their favorite music and why they like it. Take notes on their answers.

2 When you return to class, report the results of your survey. Teach your classmates any new words you learned for talking about music. Tell whether the words have a positive or negative connotation.

Part Two: On the Phone

A. Prelistening

DISCUSSION

You will hear a conversation about buying concert tickets. Before you listen, discuss the following questions with a partner or in a small group.

- When was the last time you attended a concert? Where was it? Who performed?
- How did you get tickets? How much did they cost? Where did you sit?
- What are some different ways of getting tickets for a concert? For example, have you ever used a ticket agency such as Ticketmaster?

VOCABULARY PREVIEW

Read the sentences. Using the context, guess the meanings of the boldfaced words and expressions. Then match them with their definitions. You will hear this vocabulary in the conversation.

1. _____ You can buy movie tickets online in order to **avoid** standing in line at the theater.

2. _____ Gary was annoyed when he called a ticket agency and they put him **on hold** for ten minutes.

3. _____ When I got a job as a customer service representative, my supervisor **monitored** my work very closely.

4. _____ Every Sunday Alice reads the paper to find out about the week's **upcoming** musical events.

5. _____ The Paul McCartney concert was **sold out** two hours after the tickets went on sale.

6. _____ We had nothing to do Friday night, so we decided to go to the symphony and try to get concert tickets **at the door**.

7. _____ We had a great view of the ballet dancers from the **orchestra section**.

8. _____ The theater has a **policy** of no refunds, exchanges, or cancellations on tickets to entertainment events.

a. the seats located on the floor of a theater (not on the balcony) and closest to the stage

b. the official rules of a company or organization

c. happening soon

d. watch carefully, listen to, or examine something over a period of time

e. at the time and place of the show

f. have no more items, such as tickets, because all of them have already been bought

g. prevent something from happening

h. waiting to speak or be spoken to on the telephone

B. Listening

MAIN IDEAS

🎧 **1** Listen to a telephone recording followed by a conversation between a customer and a customer service representative. Circle the words that complete the statements correctly. After listening, discuss your answers with a partner.

1. The recording gives information on buying tickets from <u>a ticket agency</u> / <u>a university ticket office</u>.

2. Tickets <u>are</u> / <u>aren't</u> still available.

3. The concert <u>will</u> / <u>won't</u> be sold out soon.

4. The caller <u>has</u> / <u>hasn't</u> decided to buy the tickets.

DETAILS AND INFERENCES

🎧 **2** Listen to the phone call again and answer the questions. Then discuss your answers with a partner.

1. If you do not wish to order tickets from the agent, you may also buy tickets

    a. at the door.

    b. on the website.

    c. at the ticket office.

2. The university monitors some phone calls because they want to

    a. know which tickets people are buying.

    b. get your name and address for advertising purposes.

    c. supervise the quality of service offered by the ticket agents.

3. Which number would you press on your telephone for the following:

   a. to order tickets for events on campus _____

   b. information about parking _____

   c. information about future events _____

4. If you have a rotary phone, you should

   a. stay on the line.

   b. hang up and call a different number.

   c. use a touch-tone phone.

5. $20 tickets are

   a. for orchestra level seats.

   b. the least expensive.

   c. not available anymore.

6. If you buy tickets and decide you don't want them, you can

   a. exchange them for tickets for future concerts.

   b. not get your money back.

   c. get your money back if you have the receipt.

LISTENING FOR LANGUAGE

3 **Read the information about stress in compound nouns.**

FOCUS ON SOUND
Stress in Compound Nouns

Compound nouns consist of two nouns that combine to form a single meaning. Normally the first word or syllable is stressed.[1]

Examples: orange juice, tablecloth.

Sometimes the two nouns are written as one word: basketball, keyboard.

At other times the two words are written separately: box office, ticket agency.

Many compound nouns are found in the dictionary.

---

[1]Reminder: Stressed words are pronounced louder and higher in pitch than unstressed words.

4 Listen to compound nouns on the recording. Repeat them after the speaker. Listen for the stressed word or syllable. Place a mark over the stressed syllable.

Example: tícket office

1. website
2. office hours
3. ticket prices

4. orchestra level
5. refund policy

5 With a partner, take turns pronouncing the following compound nouns. Check your partner's pronunciation.

rock music
nightclub
music teacher
tape recorder
CD player

string instruments
concert hall
piano lesson
jazz musician
radio station

C. Real Talk: Use What You've Learned

VOCABULARY REVIEW: PAIR INTERVIEW

Work in pairs. Each student should look at one of the boxes below. Take turns asking and answering questions with the boldfaced vocabulary from Part Two.

STUDENT A's QUESTIONS

1. When you go to a concert, how do you usually buy your ticket: on the phone, online, in person at a ticket office, or **at the door**?

2. What's the top price you would pay for a ticket in the **orchestra section** to see your favorite performer?

3. Have you ever found a way to get tickets to a concert that was **sold out**?

ROLE PLAY

Imagine that the rock band Coldplay is coming to perform in your city. You and five friends are interested in going to their show. With a partner, role play a telephone call between a caller and a ticket agent at the concert hall. Student A: Look at the information below. Student B: Look at the information on page 86. Use correct stress for compound nouns.

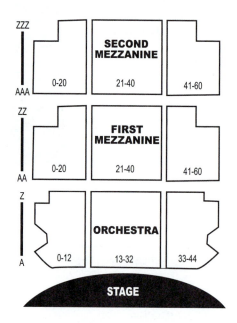

COMPOUND NOUN TREASURE HUNT

As you watch TV or listen to the radio, write a list of compound nouns you hear. Bring your list to class and share it with your classmates. Hold a competition to see which student collects the most compound nouns.

Part Three: On the Air

A. Prelistening

DISCUSSION

You will hear a report about music file-sharing. Before you listen, discuss the following questions with a partner or in a small group.

1. Where do you prefer to get your music? Look at the list of music sources below. Discuss your choices and your reasons.

   • buy CDs

   • listen to the radio

   • listen on the Internet

   • download music onto my computer

   • download music and save it on CDs or on my MP3 player

2. If you chose downloading, do you ever worry about doing something illegal?

VOCABULARY PREVIEW

Read the sentences. Using the context, guess the meanings of the boldfaced words and expressions. Then match them with their definitions. You will hear this vocabulary in the report.

1. _____ The **recording industry** produces over $3 billion a year in music sales.

2. _____ When a newspaper told lies about Elton John, he **sued** them for £350,000.

3. _____ Police are investigating a **threat** made against Madonna by a crazy fan.

4. _____ If people don't pay their taxes, the government will **come after** them.

5. _____ I like all these songs, but the last **track** is my favorite.

6. _____ Music companies try to **crack down on** illegal downloading.

7. _____ Singers become rich only if a **significant** number of people buy their music.

8. _____ Even though the weather was terrible, the fans **shrugged off** the rain and stayed for the whole concert.

9. _____ One mistake probably won't **detract from** an artist's success, but many mistakes will.

10. _____ A good singer **deserves** to get good pay.

---

a. one of the songs or pieces of music on a CD

b. take strong action to stop a problem

c. make a legal complaint against someone in court, especially for money, because they harmed you in some way

d. large enough to be noticeable

e. not worry about

f. a statement that you will cause someone pain, unhappiness, or trouble

g. look for someone in order to punish him or her; pursue

h. companies that produce and sell music

i. earn something by good or bad actions

j. take away from, reduce the quality

B. Listening

MAIN IDEAS

🎧 ❶ Listen to a radio report about sharing music files on the Internet. Answer the following questions.

1. What is the recording industry trying to do?

   _____

2. How do most college students in the radio report feel about this?

   _____

DETAILS AND INFERENCES

🎧 ❷ Listen to the radio report again. Answer the questions based on the information in the report.

1. Who is the recording industry trying to catch?

   a. only file-sharing software companies

   b. everyone who downloads free music

   c. only people who download and share large numbers of songs

2. Why aren't Christian and Judy worried about lawsuits?

    a. It's impossible to crack down on millions of people.

    b. They don't download a significant number of songs.

    c. The punishment is very light.

3. Why do they say they download instead of buying music?

    a. MP3 players are very cheap.

    b. Buying music is too expensive.

    c. They feel guilty about spending too much money on CDs.

4. What is Chris Robeson's opinion?

    a. He agrees with Christian and Judy.

    b. He thinks file sharing is wrong.

    c. He thinks musicians make enough money from other sources.

LISTENING FOR LANGUAGE

3 Read the information about stress in phrasal verbs.

FOCUS ON SOUND
Stress on Phrasal Verbs

Phrasal verbs consist of a verb and one or two prepositions, which combine to form a single meaning. In phrasal verbs, the *second* word gets the stress.

Examples: turn óff, fill óut, take cáre of

4 Listen to phrasal verbs from the recording. Repeat them after the speaker. Mark the stressed word. The first one is done for you.

    1. come áfter   4. come out

    2. pull out of   5. shrug off

    3. turn off   6. crack down on

5 The following sentences include phrasal verbs and compound nouns. With a partner, mark the stressed words in the underlined phrases. Then take turns reading the sentences aloud.

1. Christian isn't worried that the <u>músic companies</u> will <u>come after</u> him for sharing <u>music files</u>.

2. Satoshi <u>turned off</u> the MP3 player that he had <u>pulled out of</u> his pocket.

3. The <u>recording industry</u> can't <u>crack down on</u> millions of <u>IP addresses</u>.

4. <u>Music fans</u> just <u>shrug off</u> the threat of <u>lawsuits</u>.

C. Real Talk: Use What You've Learned

VOCABULARY REVIEW: DISCUSSION

Work in small groups. Discuss the following questions. Remember to use the vocabulary in the box below and the boldfaced expressions from Part Three.

come after	detract from	significant
crack down on	recording industry	threat
deserve	shrugged off	track

1. With whom do you agree in the radio report—the students or the **recording industry**? What's your main reason?

2. Is there a **significant** difference between stealing a product from a store and downloading music without paying for it? Explain your answer.

3. Are the following activities illegal in your country? If so, how do companies in your country **crack down** on them?
   - downloading music from the Internet
   - copying TV programs
   - selling "bootleg" (illegally copied) CDs, videotapes, and DVDs
   - copying complete or large parts of books
   - selling fake (illegally copied) designer items: clothes, shoes, bags, and so on

4. Who **deserves** to be sued for the activities in item 3: the seller, the buyer, or nobody? Give reasons for your opinion.

5. Does the **threat** of getting caught and sued keep you from downloading music illegally?

MOCK TRIAL

1 Imagine that "Judy" from the radio interview is sued for illegally downloading songs from the Internet. Follow the steps below to debate Judy's case. Divide into three groups:

- Judy's defense lawyers
- the recording company's lawyers
- the judges

PREPARATION

2 Work in your groups.

- Lawyers: Prepare a list of arguments to support your side. Use the appropriate form below.

Arguments in Judy's Defense
Recording companies and artists make huge profits.

Arguments in Recording Companies' Defense
Artists deserve to get paid for their work.

- Judges: Prepare to hear both sides of the argument. Discuss what points each side might present. For example, how will each side define *stealing*?

PRESENTATION

3 Follow the steps to present your arguments.

1. Each team of lawyers chooses two speakers to present their side to the class.
2. Conduct the "trial" as follows:
    - First lawyer for the recording companies presents arguments.
    - Judy's first lawyer presents arguments.
    - Second lawyer for the recording companies responds to Judy's lawyer and concludes.
    - Judy's second lawyer responds and concludes.

4 Judges should listen and take notes during the whole trial. Afterwards they should decide if Judy is "guilty" or "not guilty." If they decide that Judy is "guilty," they should decide what her punishment will be.

Part Four: In Class

A. Prelistening

QUIZ: *Rap Music*

1 How much do you know about rap music? Take the following quiz and find out! Mark the statements *T* (True) or *F* (False). Then check your answers on page 99.

_____ 1. *Rap* is a 1960s informal word meaning "conversation."

_____ 2. Rap music originated in Chicago.

_____ 3. The first rap songs appeared in the 1950s.

_____ 4. Approximately 75 percent of the people who listen to rap music in America are white.

_____ 5. Rap lyrics always contain political messages.

_____ 6. Taking a section of one recording and reusing it in a new recording is called *sampling*.

_____ 7. When speaking about music, the terms *rap* and *hip-hop* mean almost the same thing.

_____ 8. Worldwide record sales of rap music are decreasing.

_____ 9. The United States and Japan are the two largest markets for rap music in the world.

2 Work in small groups. Share what you know about the questions in the quiz.

VOCABULARY PREVIEW

Read the sentences. Using the context, guess the meanings of the boldfaced words and expressions. Then match them with their definitions. You will hear this vocabulary in the lecture.

1. _____ The rap singer clapped his hands and moved with the rhythm as he **chanted** the lyrics to his song.

2. _____ The main **components** of pop music are the melody and the lyrics.

3. ____ With its unusual rhythms and free form, modern jazz is one of the most **sophisticated** types of music. Many people do not appreciate it.

4. ____ One of the most **prominent** twentieth-century American composers of classical music was Aaron Copland.

5. ____ Rock 'n' roll **emerged** in the United States in the 1950s and exploded in popularity through the songs of Elvis Presley.

6. ____ Expensive cars, clothes, and jewelry are a few of the **status symbols** commonly displayed by popular rap singers.

7. ____ These days some famous singers use their popularity to **promote** useful causes such as antismoking campaigns or AIDS awareness.

8. ____ In the twenty-first century, rap music has entered the **mainstream**. People of all ages, races, and social classes listen to it.

9. ____ The rap artist Eminem is a musical **phenomenon**. Although he is white, he is the most popular rap singer in the world.

---

a. appear or come out from

b. repeat a word or phrase again and again

c. an exceptional or unusual thing, event, or person

d. very advanced, or working in a complicated way

e. objects that show off the owner's wealth or high social position

f. try to persuade people to support an idea or a way of doing things

g. common or accepted way of thinking or behaving in a society

h. parts

i. well-known and important

B. Listening and Note-Taking

LECTURE ORGANIZATION: CLASSIFYING

1 Read the following information about classification.

A common way of organizing information is by dividing a large topic into smaller classes, types, or categories. Music, for example, can be divided into many types, including classical, rock, folk, country, and so on.

A speaker may use the following expressions to signal this method of organization:

• Music can be	divided	into many	categories.
	classified		types.
	broken down		groups.
			classes.
			genres.

OR

• There are many **types / categories / groups/ components** of music.

2 Listen to the sentences and take notes. The first one is done for you.

(*Note:* The abbreviation *e.g.* means "for example.")

a. <u>Jazz—dozens of types, e.g., Latin, Dixieland, free, ragtime</u>

b. _____

_____

_____

c. _____

_____

_____

d. _____

_____

_____

LECTURE LANGUAGE: PARAPHRASING

3 Read the following information about paraphrasing.

> *To paraphrase* means "to restate an idea in a shorter or clearer way." Lecturers frequently introduce an important term or complex idea and then paraphrase it in order to make sure listeners understand it and have time to write it down.
>
> Some words and expressions that signal a paraphrase when speaking are:
>
> In other words,
>
> To put it another way,
>
> I mean,
>
> or*
>
> That is to say,
>
> Example: My tastes in music are somewhat out of the ordinary. *That is to say*, no one I know likes the same kind of music I do.
>
> ---
>
> *used for restating one word or a phrase, e.g.: Folk music is a very American kind, *or* genre, of music.

4 Listen to lecture excerpts containing paraphrasing. Fill in the paraphrase signals you hear.

1. Why is it that when we hear a rap song, whether it's in English or Farsi or Korean or French, we immediately know that it's rap? _____, what are the elements or characteristics that make this style of music so distinctive, so easy to recognize?

2. Well, rap can be defined as a genre of music consisting of rhyming lyrics that are spoken or chanted over a musical background. _____, the two essential components of rap are (1) rhyming lyrics and (2) musical accompaniment.

3. Now the background melody, _____ the tune, is the part that you can sing. And it can be created using any instrument or combination of instruments. Typically, though, in a rap song the melody is not the most prominent _____ memorable element.

4. The most prominent element is the backbeat, _____ the rhythm.

TAKING NOTES

🎧 ⑤ Listen to the lecture. Take notes on your own paper. Then look at the outline below. It includes the main ideas and some details from the lecture. Use your notes to complete the outline. Use the margin notes to help you.

introduction	Topic:
	Why easy to recognize?
	◯
definition	Rap:
(2 components)	
origins of rap	1970s:
	◯
	Musical elements today:
	1.
	2. (most prominent)
	◯
	3.

(continued)

other components of rap	Lyrics:
○	1.
	2.
○	These days:
○	
conclusion	

REVIEWING THE LECTURE

6 Work with a partner or in a small group. Use your notes to discuss the following questions.

1. What elements of rap music make it so easy to recognize?
2. What did you learn about the history of rap music?
3. What is the difference between the two types of rap lyrics?
4. What has happened to rap music since the mid-1990s?

C. Real Talk: Use What You've Learned

VOCABULARY REVIEW: INTERVIEW

Answer the following questions which include boldfaced vocabulary from Part Four. Then interview your parents or someone from their generation. Compare the answers and report the differences to your class.

	Your Answers	Older Generation's Answers
Who is the most **prominent** singer or musician of your generation?		
When you were in high school, did your parents like the music you listened to? Was your music in the **mainstream** at that time?		
Should the government remove any shocking **components** of lyrics? Or do you think that "warning labels" on CDs are enough?		
Do you think that singers and musicians should use their status to **promote** political ideas?		

ORAL REPORT

Prepare a three- to five-minute report on a rap singer or rap song you know well.[3] Use Part Four vocabulary from the box below in your talk. In addition, use expressions for classifying and paraphrasing if appropriate. If you own a recording of this song or by this artist, bring it to class and play it with your presentation.

chant	mainstream	promote
component	phenomenon	sophisticated
emerge	prominent	status symbol

ANSWERS TO THE QUIZ FROM PRELISTENING ON PAGE P. 92

1. T
2. F (It originated in New York City.)
3. F (Rap began in the 1970s.)
4. T (as of 2003)
5. F (They contain a variety of messages.)
6. T
7. T
8. F (As of 2003 they are increasing.)
9. F (It's the United States and France.)

---

[3]The Internet has information on rap music in most countries. Use a search engine such as Google or Yahoo and perform a search for "rap + [your country/language]," for example, "rap + Indonesian."

CHAPTER 5

Getting the Job Done

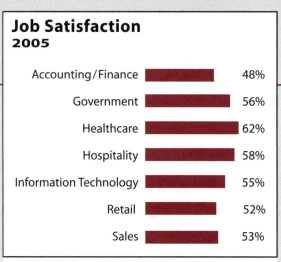

Job Satisfaction
2005

Accounting/Finance	48%
Government	56%
Healthcare	62%
Hospitality	58%
Information Technology	55%
Retail	52%
Sales	53%

Source: The Pulse: A Quarterly Forecast on Hiring Trends and Job Changes. Used with permission of CareerBuilders.com.

Part One:
In Person

A. Prelistening

DISCUSSION

You will hear a conversation between two people about their worst jobs. Before you listen, discuss the following questions with a partner or in a small group.

- Describe a job you have had and its responsibilities. What did you like about the job? What didn't you like?

VOCABULARY PREVIEW

Read the sentences. Using the context, guess the meanings of the boldfaced words and expressions. Then match them with their definitions. You will hear this vocabulary in the conversation.

1. _____ When I was in college, I had a summer job in a department store. My job was to **promote** a new kind of makeup.

2. _____ Health workers must wash their hands frequently to get rid of **bacteria** that can make people sick.

3. _____ I ordered a set of dishes online, but the **packaging** was defective and when the dishes arrived, several plates were broken.

4. _____ While going to school in the daytime, Mr. Jiao worked as a **janitor** at night. After cleaning buildings for 10 years, he graduated from college and got a job as a math teacher.

5. _____ The drug manufacturer did not take enough time to **perfect** its new medicine; consequently, many people became sick when they used it.

6. _____ By combining her pants, shirts, shoes, and jewelry in different ways, Gail is able to wear a unique **outfit** nearly every day.

7. _____ Factory workers are usually paid by the hour, so they must **punch the clock** when coming and going.

8. _____ I spilled ketchup on my favorite dress, and although I **scrubbed** it for five minutes, I could not get it clean.

9. _____ After college I spent a year doing volunteer work in a poor neighborhood. I didn't make any money, but it was a very **worthwhile** experience.

10. _____ My brother is not a very **philosophical** person. He doesn't spend time thinking deeply about his life.

---

a. microscopic living things that may cause infection or illness

b. having the habit of thinking a lot about things

c. set of clothes worn together

d. someone whose job is to clean and take care of a building

e. make sure people know about something by advertising or offering it

f. bags, boxes, or other materials that contain a product to be sold

g. improve something until it is as good as it can be

h. useful, beneficial, profitable

i. rub something hard in order to clean it

j. record the time that you arrive at work by putting a card into a special machine (informal)

B. Listening

MAIN IDEAS

🎧 ① Listen to two friends, Bonnie and Mike, talking about their worst jobs. Fill in the chart. Then work with a partner and compare answers.

	Bonnie	Mike
Job		
Responsibilities		
Why it was a bad job		

DETAILS AND INFERENCES

② Circle the letter of the correct answer to each of the following questions. Write the clues that helped you choose your answer. Then work with a partner and compare answers.

Question	Clues
1. Bonnie hates yogurt. a. True (b.) False	She says she <u>used</u> to hate yogurt.
2. The yogurt made the runners sick because a. something was wrong with it. b. they ate it too quickly after running. c. it contained blueberries.	
3. Which of the following statements are *not* true about the yogurt packaging? a. It was new. b. It was perfect. c. It was not perfect.	

(continued)

Question	Clues

4. When Bonnie says that the yogurt went "straight down," she means that
    a. the yogurt was very thick.
    b. it fell to the ground.
    c. it spilled on people's clothes.	

5. Who lived in the place where Mike worked?
    a. vampires
    b. old people
    c. janitors	

6. While he was doing his job, Mike was the only person in the building.
    a. True
    b. False	

7. Bonnie says Mike was "like a vampire" because
    a. in his job he had to clean up blood.
    b. he worked at night and slept during the day.
    c. he was cruel to the people he worked with.	

8. Mike says his job was depressing because it made him feel
    a. worthwhile.
    b. philosophical.
    c. weird.	

9. One good thing about Mike's job was that
    a. he worked alone.
    b. he met nice people.
    c. the pay was good.	

LISTENING FOR LANGUAGE

3 Read the following information about intonation.

FOCUS ON SOUND
Intonation

Intonation refers to the way in which the level of a speaker's voice rises and falls in order to add meaning to a phrase. Intonation is used in many ways in English.

Use	Intonation
• *Yes / No* questions	Rising
Example: Do you like blueberries?	
• *Wh-* questions	Rising / falling
Example: What was your favorite job?	
• To indicate more information is coming	Rising or flat
Example: When I was in high school, I had a job in a seafood restaurant.	
• To indicate the end of a statement, speaking turn, or story.	Falling
Example: I always smelled like fish.	

4 Listen again to parts of the conversation. Listen for the intonation of the underlined words. Draw rising ⬈ or falling ⬊ arrows over the words to show the direction of the intonation. The first two items are done as examples.

Bonnie: There was a time where I really hated <u>yogurt</u>.
₁

Mike: <u>Yogurt</u>? What's wrong with <u>yogurt</u>?
₂ ₃

Bonnie: Probably <u>nothing</u>, except you know when I was in <u>college</u>, um, during the
₄ ₅
summer, I had a summer <u>job</u> and I was promoting yogurt for a major <u>corporation</u>
₆ ₇
. . . And then, the packaging was <u>new</u>. So one time I was in Beverly Hills promoting
₈
this yogurt, handing people this yogurt, and the bottoms would fall out on the
<u>packaging</u> 'cause it had not been <u>perfected</u>. And all over these . . . the, you know these
₉ ₁₀
beautiful couture <u>outfits</u> . . . this yogurt went straight <u>down</u>.
₁₁ ₁₂

Mike: Was it <u>colorful</u>?
13

Bonnie: It was beautiful, especially the <u>blueberry</u>. Oh, that had to be the <u>worst</u>.
14   15

5 Work with a partner and compare answers for Exercise 4.

6 Listen again and read along with the recording. Imitate the speaker's rising or falling intonation.

7 Read the following information about reacting to interesting, surprising, or amusing information.

CONVERSATION TOOLS

Expressing Interest, Surprise, or Amusement

In the listening, Bonnie and Mike use several of the expressions below to show interest, surprise, or amusement. Such expressions encourage speakers to continue talking.

Are you serious?	Wow!
Oh no!	You're kidding!
No way!	Oh my gosh!

8 Listen to parts of the conversation. Fill in the blanks with the expressions of interest, surprise, or amusement that you hear. Then listen again and draw arrows to show what intonation the speaker used for these expressions.

1. **Bonnie:** . . . after the runners were through running their twenty-six miles, we would hand them a yogurt, and they would eat it really quickly . . . and they would just throw it back, and drink it down, eat it whatever, and then, oh . . .

   Mike: _____?

   Bonnie: They would get sick!

2. **Mike:** The worst job I ever had? I was the night janitor at a, um, at an old people's home once a long time ago.

   Bonnie: _____!

3. **Mike:** And the place would clear out, and I'm in this big empty facility and I'd have to go around with my little brush 'n scrub out all the toilets.

   Bonnie: _____!

   Mike: Yeah.

C. Real Talk: Use What You've Learned

VOCABULARY REVIEW: QUESTIONS AND ANSWERS

Work in pairs. Each student should choose one of the boxes below. Take turns asking and answering questions with the boldfaced vocabulary from Part Two. Express interest, surprise, or amusement when appropriate.

STUDENT A's QUESTIONS

1. Would you ever accept a job **promoting** a low-quality product, like Bonnie did? Why or why not?

2. Have you ever had a job where you had to **punch the clock**? Did you like it?

3. Why did Mike say his job was **worthwhile**? Do you agree with him?

4. Where would you shop if you wanted to buy an **outfit** to wear to a formal party?

STUDENT B's QUESTIONS

1. Have you ever bought a product just because you liked the **packaging**?

2. Are you trying to **perfect** your English pronunciation? What techniques are you using?

3. In your country, are **janitors** usually men, women, or both?

4. Are you a **philosophical** person? If yes, in what way?

DISCUSSION: JOB PRIORITIES

1 What is important to you in a job? Read the items in the chart. Put a check (✓) in the column that matches your opinion.

	Very Important	Important	Not Very Important
Working alone			
Working with a team of people			
Doing different things every day			

(continued)

	Very Important	Important	Not Very Important
Working outdoors			
Helping people			
Making a lot of money			
Managing or supervising people			
Having the power to make independent decisions			
Using my hands to create a product			
Solving difficult problems			
Using technology in my work			
Having a flexible schedule			
Feeling excited about my work			

2 In small groups, tell your classmates about your preferences. Use expressions of interest, surprise, or amusement when appropriate.

1. Which items are very important to you?
2. Does your job now, or will the job you will have in the future, match the items that are very important to you?

ORAL PRESENTATION

1 Prepare a one- to two-minute talk on your best or worst job. (If you have never had a job, you may talk about a class, birthday, or vacation.) Include a story to illustrate why it was good or bad. Practice your talk at home. Plan where you will use intonation to signal that your story is either continuing or finished.

2 In class, sit in groups of four or five. Take turns presenting your talks. Listeners should respond with expressions of interest, amusement, or surprise. Be sure to use correct intonation in your responses.

Part Two: On the Phone

A. Prelistening

DISCUSSION

You will hear a conversation between a job applicant and a receptionist, and another between the job applicant and the employer. Before you listen, work with a partner to complete the task and discuss the question.

1. The list below contains steps taken by North Americans who are searching for a job. Place the activities in order.

_____ go for an interview

_____ call a company

_____ wait for an answer

_____ find out about the job (from an ad or a friend)

_____ make an appointment for an interview

_____ follow up (by mail / e-mail / phone)

_____ send in a résumé

2. How is the process of looking for a job similar or different in your country or culture?

VOCABULARY PREVIEW

Read the sentences. Using the context, guess the meanings of the boldfaced words and expressions. Then match them with their definitions. You will hear this vocabulary in the conversations.

1. _____ You should **follow up** a job interview by writing a thank-you note the next day.

2. _____ Your **résumé** should include your language skills in addition to your college degrees and employment history.

3. _____ The workers at the university housing office come from **diverse** countries, cultures, and backgrounds.

4. _____ John has just graduated from college, so he doesn't have the **qualifications** to be a manager.

5. _____ I know a lawyer whose **clients** pay her $350 per hour.

6. _____ Nora quit her job because she didn't like to **deal with** rude customers.

7. _____ In some industries, being a salesperson **involves** a lot of traveling and long hours away from home.

8. _____ Mr. Kim's secretary takes care of his **correspondence** because he is too busy to read his mail.

9. _____ People who are responsible for their company's **billing** should have strong math skills.

10. _____ Some people are very good at **multitasking**, such as reading their e-mail while talking on the phone.

11. _____ Jim's **commute** from the suburbs to downtown takes an hour every day.

---

a. skills or experience needed for a particular job or position

b. customers who pay for services or advice

c. includes something as a necessary part or result

d. sending and receiving letters

e. requests for payment for a company's products or services

f. the ability to do more than one job at a time

g. regular travel to get to work

h. take additional action at a later time

i. interact with someone, or have a business connection

j. very different from each other

k. a one- or two-page summary of your education and work experience

B. Listening

MAIN IDEAS

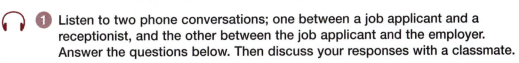 Listen to two phone conversations; one between a job applicant and a receptionist, and the other between the job applicant and the employer. Answer the questions below. Then discuss your responses with a classmate.

1. Why is the man calling the company?

_____

2. What does Ms. Baker want to know about Mr. Williams?

_____

_____

_____

3. What will probably happen next?

_____

DETAILS AND INFERENCES

2 Listen again. Mark the statements *T* (true) or *F* (false).

_____ 1. Scott is applying for several positions.

_____ 2. Ms. Baker has not had time to read Scott's résumé.

_____ 3. Scott quit his job at the university because it was too stressful.

_____ 4. Scott has strong qualifications.

_____ 5. Ms. Baker is worried about the distance Scott has to travel to work.

LISTENING FOR LANGUAGE

3 Read the information in the box to learn more about intonation.

FOCUS ON SOUND:
Rising Intonation Signaling Hesitation

Rising or level intonation at the end of a statement can indicate that a speaker is hesitant, uncertain, or lacks confidence, especially when answering questions.

Example:

Scott: Oh, well, I'm just calling to follow up on my job application. I sent . . .

I faxed in my résumé last week and I just . . .

Receptionist: For which position? We have several . . .

Scott: Oh, the administrative assistant.

To sound confident and convincing, be sure to use falling intonation at the ends of statements.

🎧 ④ Listen again to parts of the conversation. Listen to Scott's intonation and decide if he sounds hesitant or certain. Circle the correct answer. Work with a partner and compare answers.

1. hesitant   certain
2. hesitant   certain
3. hesitant   certain
4. hesitant   certain
5. hesitant   certain

C. Real Talk: Use What You've Learned

VOCABULARY REVIEW: DISCUSSION

Work in small groups. Discuss the following questions. Remember to use the boldfaced expressions from Part Two.

1. Why do employers in some countries require a photograph with a **résumé**? Why do you think this is rarely done in the United States?

2. If you got no response from a company after applying for a job, would you **follow up** or just forget about it?

3. Besides education and work experience, what **qualifications** are necessary to be a good manager?

4. Name some jobs that include a lot of **multitasking**. What might be the disadvantages of doing more than one job at a time?

5. What's the best way to **deal with** a difficult boss?

6. What is the longest **commute** (in time or distance) that you would be willing to have?

7. In your future job, will you need to **deal with** a **diverse** group of clients?

8. Would you want a job that **involves** a lot of travelling?

9. What kinds of jobs require a worker to take care of **correspondence**? How about **billing**?

ROLE PLAY

Work with a partner. Role play one of the phone conversations below. Use rising and falling intonation to show hesitation or certainty. Perform your role play for the class.

	Applicant	Interviewer
Scenario 1	• sent in résumé and is now making a follow-up call • tries hard to "sell" himself or herself and becomes a little pushy • insists on setting up an interview appointment	• hasn't read the résumé yet • refuses to schedule an interview until he or she has read the résumé • promises to call applicant next week
Scenario 2	• résumé has gaps; that is, several years of employment history are missing • is hesitant but tries to explain the gaps honestly	• wants to know about the gaps in the résumé • after listening to applicant's explanation, decides whether or not to schedule an interview
Scenario 3	• isn't sure he or she wants the job anymore • wants to know more details about the job, especially the benefits; then decides whether or not to schedule an interview	• likes applicant's résumé and is eager to set up an interview • does his or her best to "sell" the job to applicant

PROBLEM SOLVING

Culture note

In the United States, it is illegal for an interviewer to ask a job applicant anything personal that is not directly job-related. For example, questions about an applicant's age, marital status, country of origin, religion, family, sexual preference, and health status are not permitted. The purpose of this law is to protect prospective employees from discrimination. Job advertisements also need to follow this law. For example, it is illegal to request a photograph or to post an ad that indicates age preference, such as "recent college graduate" or "age 25–35 preferred."

Work in groups. You are the human resources manager of Metro Hotels, Inc. You want to be sure that your company obeys the law against discrimination in hiring. Read the advertisement your company placed for a position. Then change the application form below to remove unfair questions. Add any questions that would be useful in selecting the best manager. Share answers with another group when you have finished.

Help Wanted

Restaurant Seeking Experienced
★ **Assistant Manager** ★

Supervise restaurant staff, handle payroll, work flexible hours (including nights and weekends)
We Offer:
Great staff, great atmosphere, excellent benefits & advancement opportunity
Base pay: $30,000-60,000/yr
Complete application at hr@metrohotels.com.Job

JOB APPLICATION FORM

METRO HOTELS

BACKGROUND INFORMATION

Name: _____
FIRST   MIDDLE   LAST

Address: _____

City: _____ State: _____ Zip: _____

How long at this address? _____ Age: _____ Sex: _____ Height: _____ Weight: _____

CITIZENSHIP INFORMATION

Citizenship: _____ U.S. _____ Other   Marital status: _____ Married _____ Single _____ Divorced

Number of children: _____ Their ages: _____

Religious Holidays Observed: _____

EMPLOYMENT INFORMATION

Previous Job: _____

Reason for leaving job: _____

Salary at previous job: _____

EDUCATION

Education (degree received): _____ Year degree completed: _____

OTHER

Date of last health exam: _____ Do you wear glasses or contact lenses? _____

Do you have any disabilities? _____ If yes, explain: _____

Have you ever been arrested? _____ If yes, give details: _____

REFERENCES _____

Part Three: On the Air

A. Prelistening

DISCUSSION

You will hear an interview about good manners at work. Before you listen, discuss the following questions with a partner or in a small group.

- In each picture, one person is behaving rudely. What is the person doing? How would you feel if you worked in an office with one of these people?

- Have you ever worked in a place where your co-workers' behavior bothered you? Describe the annoying behavior.

VOCABULARY PREVIEW

Read the sentences. Using the context, guess the meanings of the boldfaced words and expressions. Then match them with their definitions. You will hear this vocabulary in the interview.

1. _____ I don't feel that it would be **proper** to call the president of my company by his first name.

2. _____ It is good **etiquette** to introduce yourself at the beginning of a job interview and to thank the interviewer at the end.

3. _____ We like doing business with that company because the staff is always **courteous** and helpful.

4. _____ Diana is a **considerate** boss. She treats workers respectfully and listens patiently to their concerns.

5. _____ Tom received a funny e-mail, so he **forwarded** it to five other friends.

6. _____ I can't tell you what my manager said because he asked me to keep it **confidential**.

7. _____ If you steal from your company, you will be **fired**.

8. _____ Jack decided to **resign** from the company because his boss refused to raise his salary.

9. _____ When Julie's salary was reduced, she **repressed** her disappointment in the office but secretly started looking for a new job.

10. _____ Try to be **poised** when talking to your manager, even if you feel nervous inside.

11. _____ Mrs. Barton quit her old job but did not **burn her bridges** by saying bad things about the company or her co-workers.

---

a. polite

b. send to another address

c. secret, private

d. leave your job or position voluntarily

e. stop yourself from showing a feeling

f. formal rules for polite behavior

g. calm and confident

h. destroy relationships; make enemies (informal)

i. correct; socially acceptable

j. forced to leave a job

k. always thinking of what other people need or want and taking care not to upset them

B. Listening

MAIN IDEAS

🎧 ① Listen to part of a radio interview with etiquette experts Peggy Post and Peter Post. List four workplace etiquette problems that they discuss. Then compare answers with a partner.

1. _____

2. _____

3. _____

4. _____

DETAILS AND INFERENCES

2 Listen again. Take notes on the experts' advice for each etiquette problem you listed in Exercise 1. Then work with a partner and compare answers.

	Advice or Proper Etiquette
1.	Ask the other person . . .
2.	
3.	
4.	The boss should . . .

LISTENING FOR LANGUAGE

3 The experts in the interview suggest asking for permission when using a speaker phone: "Do you mind if I use a speaker phone?" There are many ways to ask, give, or deny permission. Study the chart below.

CONVERSATION TOOLS:
Asking, Granting, and Denying Permission

Asking Permission	Granting	Denying	
May / could / can I . . .	Certainly.	I'd rather you didn't.	**polite**
Would it be possible for me to . . .	Of course.	I'm afraid not / that's not possible.	
Is it OK if I . . .	Be my guest.	I don't think you should.	
	Go right ahead.	Sorry, no.	
	No problem.	I'm sorry, you can't.	
	Sure.	Forget it.	
		Don't even think about it.	**rude**
Do / Would you mind if I . .	No, I don't mind.	Yes, I do mind.	
Would it bother you if I . . .	Not at all.	Yes, it would bother me.	

4 Work with a partner. Think of situations in which it is polite to ask people for permission at work. Use expressions for asking, granting, and denying permission. Take turns being Speaker A and Speaker B.

Speaker A: You want to do something that might bother your co-workers. Ask for permission to do it.

Speaker B: Either give or deny permission.

Example:

A: Would it be OK if I went ahead of you on the copy machine? I just have one page.

B: Sure, go right ahead.

Culture note

According to a survey of 1,500 office workers in England, the top five most annoying office habits are the following:

- getting e-mail from people sitting in the same office
- colleague's choice of radio station
- colleagues who don't share the tea-making duties
- colleagues listening to voicemails on speaker phone
- people who swear at their computer

Source: *Coventry Evening Telegraph*, July 17, 2003

C. Real Talk: Use What You've Learned

VOCABULARY REVIEW: DISCUSSION

Work in small groups. The chart on the next page lists situations common in most jobs. Describe the courteous and inconsiderate behavior for each circumstance. Then discuss the questions that follow the chart. Remember to use the boldfaced expressions from Part Three.

Situation	Courteous Behavior	Inconsiderate Behavior
a. using a copy machine	letting others in line go first if they have less to copy.	leaving the paper tray empty.
b. letting your company / boss know that you'll be absent		
c. quitting your job		
d. arriving late at a meeting		
e. borrowing office supplies from a co-worker		
f. eating lunch in a shared office		
g. talking on the telephone		
h. forwarding e-mail		

1. What is the **proper** workplace **etiquette** for the situations above?

2. What conditions might cause you to **resign** from a job you like?

3. Why is it important not to **burn bridges** when leaving a job?

4. What would you do if a co-worker shared some **confidential** information with you about your company's illegal activities?

5. As a boss, would you **fire** an employee who has excellent job skills but is rude and **inconsiderate**?

S U R V E Y

Interview three English speakers about their work. Follow these steps.

1. Ask the following questions: (a) Where do you work? (b) Do you have a pet peeve concerning your co-workers' workplace behavior?

2. Take notes in the chart below.

	Place of Work	Pet Peeve
Respondent 1		
Respondent 2		
Respondent 3		

3. Share your survey results with your class. Use some of the expressions of annoyance you learned in Chapter 2 (page 32). What were the five most irritating activities?

Part Four: In Class

A. Prelistening

DISCUSSION

You will hear a lecture about why Americans work hard. Before you listen, study the information below, and discuss the questions that follow in small groups.

Annual Average Hours Worked in 2002, Selected Countries	
Country	Average Hours
South Korea	2,447
Japan	1,848
Australia	1,824
United States	1,815
Canada	1,778
Ireland	1,668
Sweden	1,625
France	1,545
Germany	1,444
Norway	1,342

Source: money.cnn.com, October 16, 2003, International Labor Organization (UN)

Vacation Days Allowed by Law, Selected Countries		
Country	Paid Vacation Days, by Law	Average Days Taken
Sweden	25	25–35
Germany	24	30
Norway	21	30
Spain	25	30
France	25	25–30
Ireland	20	28
Australia	20	25
China	15	15
Japan	10	17.5
United States	0	10.2

Source: abcnews.com, June 25, 2003

• Write three facts from the charts that you find surprising or interesting.

_____

_____

_____

• Based on the information in the charts, how much do Americans work compared to workers in Asia and Europe?

• Why do Americans work so hard, in your opinion?

VOCABULARY PREVIEW

Read the sentences. Using the context, guess the meanings of the boldfaced words and expressions. Then match them with their definitions. You will hear this vocabulary in the lecture.

1. _____ What **accounts for** Mila's poor attitude at work lately? Is she having a problem with her boss?

2. _____ A basic **principle** of the U.S. workforce is that men and women should get equal pay for the same job.

3. _____ At the end of the year, many companies **reward** their employees for their hard work with a cash gift.

4. _____ That store sells men's suits in a wide **range** of prices, from several thousand dollars to just a few hundred.

5. _____ In this clothing factory, workers' **wages** are based on skill and years of experience.

6. _____ In some countries there is a large **disparity** between men's and women's salaries, even in the same profession.

7. _____ As an **incentive** to its sales team, the company promises a free trip to Hawaii to the person who sells the most computers in a month.

8. _____ Heavy traffic **led to** long delays on the freeway this morning.

9. _____ I took the job with the university because of its outstanding salary and **benefits**.

---

a. a difference or gap between two things, especially an unfair one

b. advantages in addition to salary, such as health insurance and retirement contributions

c. something that encourages a person to want to work harder

d. caused; resulted in

e. a basic rule

f. give something to someone for doing something good or helpful

g. explain the reason for something

h. the distance between two extremes; for example, the distance between the highest and lowest points

i. money paid for work; a salary

B. Listening and Note-Taking

LECTURE ORGANIZATION: CAUSE AND EFFECT

1 Read the following information about cause-and-effect organization.

> Speakers frequently talk about the causes (reasons) and effects (results) of a situation, event, or problem. The lecture may focus on the reasons, the results, or both. The speaker may also speak about the solution(s) to the problem. A well-organized speaker will state the focus of the lecture in the introduction.
>
> The notes for a cause-and-effect lecture might be organized like this example:

```
I. Prob: Children watching too much TV
II. Causes
        A. Parents busy—use TV as a "babysitter"
        B. Children home alone—no adult supervision
III. Effects
        A. No exercise → overweight
        B. Poor reading skills
        C. Weak eyes
```

2 Listen to the lecture introduction. Check the focus of the lecture.

_____ causes

_____ effects

_____ solutions

LECTURE LANGUAGE: CAUSE AND EFFECT

3 Read the following information about structures for talking about cause and effect. There are many ways of expressing cause and effect in English. Some of the common ones are listed below.

Expressions Signaling Cause

Because / Since the holidays are coming, department stores are hiring more staff.[1]

Because of / Due to the new trade laws, thousands of workers will lose their jobs.[2]

Many U.S. companies are moving overseas. The **cause / reason** is the high cost of production in the United States.

In the United States, **if** people lose their jobs, they often lose their health insurance.

The cost of labor has gone up 30 percent. **As a result / Therefore,** we will need to raise the price of our product.

Housing prices are high, **so** some people have to work two jobs in order to pay their bills.

An increase in the price of oil **resulted in / led to** higher gasoline prices.

One cause of poverty is lack of education.

Lack of education **causes** poverty.

When taking notes on causes and effects, most people write the cause first. Note the use of abbreviations and symbols in these examples:

dept. stores hiring staff b/c of holidays

high housing prices ➔ people work 2 jobs

if people lose jobs ➔ lose health ins.

---

[1]It is also possible to reverse the order of the clauses: "Department stores are hiring more staff because / since the holidays are coming."
[2]Or, "Thousands of workers will lose their jobs because of / due to the new trade laws."

🎧 ④ **Listen to sentences from the lecture. Fill in the blanks with the missing expressions of cause or effect.**

1. And compared to Europeans, well, Americans work three to four hundred hours a year more than people in Western Europe. They take fewer vacations and they retire at a later age. Why is this? How _____ that?

2. But _____ why Americans work as hard . . . why Americans work hard is that the U.S. economic structure rewards them for it, and Americans see this as a good thing.

3. In other words, people work harder _____ they know that in most cases the hard work will _____ higher pay.

4. In Europe, on the other hand, the wage gap, I mean the difference in salary between the highest and the lowest salaries in the company, is generally much smaller than in the U.S., _____ people in Europe have less of an incentive to work hard.

5. Technology actually _____ people to work more than they did twenty or thirty years ago.

TAKING NOTES

🎧 ⑤ Listen to the lecture. Take notes on your own paper. Then look at the outline below. Use your notes to complete the outline. Use the margin notes to help you.

topic

intro

-Amer. work as many hrs. as Jap. + Kor.

- " " 300–400 hrs./yr. > than West. Euro

-

-

Reasons

1. Historical: Euros. who settled U.S. = relig. Christians

believed in value of hard work

that value → until today

2. Main reason

U.S. wide range of sal.

e.g.: Pres. of U.S. co. earns 50–100 × av. wkr. →

incentives to work harder, i.e., work hard → higher pay

Europe:

3.

benefits = med insurance, unemp. ins., retirement

Europe:

U.S.:

4.

positive reason

5.

summary

REVIEWING THE LECTURE

6 Work with one or more classmates. Use your notes to restate the six reasons why Americans work hard. Did any of the information surprise you? Use a variety of expressions that signal cause and effect in your sentences.

C. Real Talk: Use What You've Learned

VOCABULARY REVIEW: DISCUSSION

Work in small groups. Discuss the following questions. Remember to use the boldfaced expressions from Part Four.

1. What **accounts for** the fact that U.S. workers have fewer vacation days than workers in most other countries?

2. In the United States, government workers get better **benefits** than workers in most private companies. Is this true in other countries that you are familiar with?

3. Did you ever receive a **reward** for outstanding performance at school or at work?

4. Look at the chart on page 126. In the year 2000, top executives at some of the largest U.S. companies earned 531 times more than the typical employee. Why do you think this huge **disparity** exists? Why is the salary **range** so much smaller in most other countries?

5. Which of the following would provide you with the best **incentive** for working harder: a higher position with more authority, a larger office, more vacation time, or a company car?

6. Would higher **wages lead** you **to** work harder?

The Global Pay Gap

Nobody beats the U.S. when it comes to the difference in pay between CEOs and the average worker. On average, CEOs at 365 of the largest publicly traded U.S. companies earned $13.1 million last year, or 531 times what the typical hourly employee took home.

Around the rest of the world, Latin America is the leader in pay disparity, though even it doesn't come close to the U.S. At the other end of the spectrum, Japan has the smallest gap between CEO and average-worker pay.

The calculations below are based on estimates by the consulting firm Towers Perrin as of Apr. 1, 2000. Average employees were assumed to be working in industrial companies with about $500 million in annual sales.

Country	CEO Compensation*	Country	CEO Compensation*	Country	CEO Compensation*
United States	531	Britain	25	New Zealand	16
Brazil	51	Thailand	23	France	16
Venezuela	54	Australia	22	Taiwan	15
South Africa	51	Netherlands	22	Sweden	14
Argentina	48	Canada	21	Germany	11
Malaysia	47	China (Shanghai)	21	South Korea	11
Mexico	45	Belgium	19	Switzerland	11
Hong Kong	38	Italy	19	Japan	10
Singapore	37	Spain	18		

* as a multiple of average employee compensation

PROBLEM SOLVING

You manage a flower shop with four employees. Business has been slow lately, and the owner has told you to let one of the workers go. But which one will you fire? Read the chart on page 127 with information about the workers. Then discuss the problem with your classmates until you reach agreement, or consensus. Use expressions in the box for reaching a consensus.

CONVERSATION TOOLS
Checking for Consensus

Do we agree?

Do we see eye to eye on this?

Are we all together on this?

Have we reached a decision?

Does anyone disagree?

Does anyone have a different point of view?

	Susanna	Tomohiro	Maggie	Hans
Age	28	24	35	21
Family	Married, one child, husband unemployed	Single	Divorced, two children in high school	Single
Education	Finished community college in the United States	Graduated from college in his country; Majored in accounting, but did not enjoy it	Finished high school in her country	College student, majoring in mathematics
Years with the company	6	3	14	1
Work performance	Punctual, honest, easy to work with; Makes occasional mistakes with customers' orders	Occasionally late because of drinking parties the night before; Artistic, makes beautiful flower arrangements	Smart, knows more than anyone about flowers and plants; Sometimes seems angry, other workers do not like her	Works quickly, never late; Cheerful, customers like him
Other information	Wants to finish college and become a nurse	Would like to stay in the flower business; Has ideas for ways to expand the company	Has been with the company since it started; The owner trusts her although they sometimes argue	His girlfriend is the daughter of the owner of the shop

CHAPTER 6

To Your Health!

Part One: In Person

A. Prelistening

DISCUSSION

You will hear a conversation about allergies. Before you listen, discuss the following questions with a partner or in a small group.

- Look at the picture. What is the woman's health problem? What are her symptoms?

- Are you, or is someone close to you, allergic to anything? What are the symptoms of this allergy? How is it treated?

- What is the best way to treat different kinds of allergies?

VOCABULARY PREVIEW

Read the sentences. Using the context, guess the meanings of the boldfaced words and expressions. Then match them with their definitions. You will hear this vocabulary in the conversation.

1. _____ Yuko's boss was not happy when she **called in sick** yesterday because she had already missed two weeks of work due to illness.

2. _____ Carlos loves bread, cakes, and pasta, so he was very **bummed out** when his doctor told him he was allergic to wheat.

3. _____ What's wrong with me? I've been feeling **out of it** for weeks. Maybe it's time to see a doctor.

4. _____ If you think you're **coming down with** a cold, you should stay in bed and drink lots of liquids.

5. _____ In spite of the medicine she takes every day, Lara's asthma has been **going from bad to worse**.

6. _____ After many tests, it **turns out** that Abdul is allergic not only to corn but also to soy.

7. _____ The doctor said, "I'm going to **prescribe** some pills for your headaches, and it's important for you to follow the instructions on the bottle carefully."

8. _____ I think it's a bad idea to take pills when you can't sleep. Why don't you try some **alternatives**, such as yoga, soft music, or a relaxing tea?

---

a. upset, disappointed (*informal*)

b. something that can be used instead of something else

c. getting sick with

d. for a doctor to say what medicine or treatment a sick person should have

e. telephone one's workplace to say that one is sick and will not be coming to work

f. feeling weak, tired, sick, or depressed (*informal*)

g. have a particular result that one did not expect

h. getting worse as time goes by

B. Listening

MAIN IDEAS

1 Listen to two colleagues, Lisa and Bene, talking about Lisa's medical problem. Take notes on the answers to the questions below.

1. Why is Lisa sad?

   _____

2. What is the cause of her problem?

   _____

3. What were her symptoms?

   _____

4. What treatment did the doctor prescribe?

   _____

5. Is there a cure for her condition?

   _____

DETAILS AND INFERENCES

Complete the exercises below. Guess if you're not sure. Then listen to the conversation again to check your answers.

2 Complete the following sentences with details from the conversation.

a. Lisa started to feel bad about _____ ago.

b. She had gotten the cat about _____ earlier.

c. Besides cats, it turns out that Lisa is also allergic to _____,

   _____ , and _____ .

d. The problem with the pills that the doctor prescribed was that they made Lisa

   feel _____ .

3 Mark the statements *T* (true) or *F* (false).

_____ a. Lisa went to the doctor as soon as she started to feel bad.

_____ b. At first Lisa thought she had a cold.

_____ c. Lisa had never spent time around cats until she got her own.

_____ d. Allergies sometimes develop into asthma.

_____ e. Lisa's treatment is helping her.

④ Circle the correct answers. There may be more than one answer.

a. Which words might logically complete Lisa's statement?

Lisa: ". . . you hear about these bad cases of asthma, and it sort of starts from these—like, you know—allergic reactions, so I was kind of . . ."

shocked   surprising   surprised   worried   sleepy   thrilled

b. Which words describe Bene's reaction to Lisa's story, in your opinion?

sad   critical   sympathetic   concerned   surprised

LISTENING FOR LANGUAGE

⑤ Read the information about thought groups and focus words.

FOCUS ON SOUND
Thought Groups and Focus Words

In English, long utterances may consist of several *thought groups*, which are short phrases or sentences. Within each thought group, one word, the *focus word*, is usually the loudest, clearest, and highest word in the phrase.[1] Normally it is the <u>last</u> content word in the phrase. Speakers often (but not always!) pause between thought groups.

Thought groups often correspond to grammatical phrases and clauses. For example (focus words are boldfaced):

Bene: . . . one of the **teachers** / called in **sick** / and I didn't have anything to **do** / this **morning**, / so they **asked** me / to come **in**.

Listening for focus words and thought groups is a strategy that can help you hear the most important information when people talk very quickly, as Lisa does.

⑥ Listen to sentences from the conversation. Underline the focus word in each thought group. The first item is done for you. After listening, practice saying the sentences with correct stress, intonation, and pauses.[2]

1. One of the <u>teachers</u> / called in <u>sick</u>, / and I didn't have anything to <u>do</u> this <u>morning</u>, / so they <u>asked</u> me to come <u>in</u>.

2. I'm just pretty bummed out. / I had to get rid of my cat.

3. I actually found out / that I was allergic.

---

[1]An utterance may have several stressed words. The focus word has the strongest stress of any word in the thought group.

[2]Remember that unstressed words are lower in pitch than stressed words, and they are often reduced. See Chapter 1, page 5.

4. About three months ago / I started feeling pretty out of it.

5. I had just gotten the cat / probably a couple of weeks before.

7 Listen to some longer sentences. Insert slashes between thought groups. Underline the focus words. After listening, practice saying the sentences with correct stress, intonation, and pauses.[3]

1. And so you went to a doctor, or . . . how did you find out whether, what were your symptoms?

2. Um, yeah, so I started, I was just feeling really lethargic, and I didn't have any energy, and you know I was sneezing a lot, and my eyes were really itchy and irritated, and I had headaches,

3. Well, at first I just thought I was just coming down with a cold.

4. Well I had told him that I had, you know, when I thought about it after a while when I couldn't figure out, you know, what possibly could be wrong, after I knew it wasn't just a cold, and I was like "Oh, I just got this cat not long before."

5. And so the doctor said, "You know, well, you know we should run some tests to see if you're allergic."

8 Read the information about ways of expressing sympathy in English.

CONVERSATION TOOLS
Expressing Sympathy

Read the following exchanges from the conversation.

Lisa: Oh yeah, it's OK, I'm just pretty bummed out. I had to get rid of my cat.

Bene: Oh no, what happened? That sounds awful.

Bene: It's too bad though that you had to lose your cat.

Lisa: Yeah, I was really bummed out about it.

Notice the expressions Bene uses to express sympathy for Lisa's loss: *Oh no, That sounds awful, It's too bad*. The following are formal and informal ways to express sympathy in English:

I'm (so, very) sorry for your loss.[4]	formal
My condolences.[5]	
I'm (so, very) sorry to hear (that).	
That's a shame. / What a shame.	
That's awful / horrible / terrible.	less formal
(That's) too bad.	
(What a) bummer. What a drag.	informal

---

[3]Incomplete or ungrammatical utterances, which are part of natural speech, may sound like thought groups, or they may be unstressed.

[4,5]Normally this expression is used to express sympathy when someone has died.

9 Work in pairs. In each situation below, Speaker B should respond to Speaker A with an appropriate expression of sympathy. Take turns playing each role.

1. Speakers A and B are classmates.

   A: I failed my final exam in U.S. history.

   B: _____.

2. Speaker A is older than Speaker B.

   A: My car was stolen last week.

   B: _____.

3. Speaker A is Speaker B's boss.

   A: I missed my flight out of Chicago and had to spend the night in the airport.

   B: _____.

4. Speaker A is married to Speaker B.

   A: I have to work late, so I won't make it home for dinner.

   B: _____.

5. Speaker A and Speaker B work together, but they do not know one another well.

   A: My grandmother died. I have to leave early to go to her funeral.

   B: _____.

6. Speaker A is a child. Speaker B is an adult.

   A: My mommy is sick. She had to go to the hospital.

   B: _____.

C. Real Talk: Use What You've Learned

VOCABULARY REVIEW: DISCUSSION

Work with a partner or in a small group. Take turns telling about an illness or medical condition that you have (now) or have had (in the past). As you talk, remember to use the Part One vocabulary from the box below. Try to divide your sentences into natural-sounding thought groups.

alternative	come down with (something)	prescribe
bummed out	go from bad to worse	turns out
call in sick	out of it	

ROLE PLAY

The chart below lists some common allergies, their symptoms, and their prevention or treatment. With a partner, choose one of the items and role play a three- to four-minute conversation. Discuss the problem, the symptoms, and the recommended treatment. Include the vocabulary from this section and expressions of sympathy.

Example:

A: Hi, _____, I haven't seen you in a while. How've you been?

B: Oh, all right, I guess.

A: You sound sad. Is something wrong?

B: Well, yes, _____.

Allergy	Symptoms	Prevention / Treatment
Wheat	Upset stomach, asthma, rash	Avoid products containing wheat.
Bee sting	Pain, swelling, nausea, fatigue, fever	Avoid wearing bright colors and perfume outdoors; if stung, take an antihistamine and pain relievers.
Peanuts	Difficulty breathing	Avoid peanuts and all products containing peanuts, including candy, ice cream, and cereals.
Mold	Sneezing, congestion, itchy and watery eyes, runny nose, and coughing	Use antihistamines, nasal spray, and allergy shots to build up immunity.
Other		

Part Two: On the Phone

Active Ingredients   **Purpose**
Diphenhydramine 25 mg. Antihistamine

Temporarily relieves runny nose, sneezing, and itchy and watery eyes due to some allergies or the common cold.

Warnings

Do not use with any other product containing diphenhydramine.

Not for use by children under 6.

Ask a doctor before use if you have glaucoma or a breathing condition.

Do not exceed the recommended dosage – excitability may occur, especially in children; marked drowsiness may occur; alcohol, sedatives, and tranquilizers may increase drowsiness; avoid alcoholic beverages; use caution when operating machinery.

A. Prelistening

DISCUSSION

You will hear a conversation at a pharmacy. Before you listen, discuss the following questions with a partner or in a small group.

- What is the purpose of the medication above?
- What medical conditions is it generally used for?
- What might happen if you exceed the recommended dosage of this medicine?
- Can this medicine be used by both adults and children?
- Have you ever used a medication like this one?

Culture note

In the United States, doctors do not provide medicines in their offices. The place to get medicines is a *pharmacy*. Some medications can be bought *over-the-counter*, meaning you can buy them without a doctor's recommendation. Other medications require a doctor's *prescription*, or written order. Prescriptions can be filled only by *pharmacists*—licensed medical professionals who, in addition to filling prescriptions, also spend time educating customers about their medications.

VOCABULARY PREVIEW

Read the sentences. Using the context, guess the meanings of the boldfaced words and expressions. Then match them with their definitions. You will hear this vocabulary in the conversation.

1. _____ When my baby developed a high fever, our **physician** told us to take him directly to the hospital.

2. _____ One **side effect** of antibiotic drugs is sensitivity to sunlight. Another one is that these drugs cause an upset stomach.

3. _____ Many medicines cause **drowsiness**, so you must not drive if you are taking them.

4. _____ Skin cancer in middle age is a **long-term** result of too much sun exposure when you are young.

5. _____ Sleeping pills can be **habit forming** if you use them every night.

6. _____ Do you know of a good natural **remedy** for treating this cough? I've had it for two weeks!

7. _____ You can grow **herbs** such as rosemary, basil, and mint in pots in your kitchen.

a. an unwanted or unexpected effect of a medicine, in addition to the main effect that the medicine is supposed to have

b. addictive; having the possibility of causing a physical dependence

c. continuing for a long time into the future

d. sleepiness

e. cure

f. plants used in cooking or in treating some medical conditions

g. a doctor

B. Listening

MAIN IDEAS

🎧 ① Listen to a pharmacist talking to a customer. Answer the questions below. Then discuss your answers with a partner.

1. Who is the caller? _____

2. Why is she calling the pharmacist? _____

3. Check (✓) all the facts that are true about Benesec, according to the pharmacist.

_____ It is used mainly for allergies.

_____ It is an antihistamine.

_____ Drowsiness is a side effect.

_____ It is habit forming.

_____ It is all right to use it every night.

_____ It is safer than plants or herbs.

D E T A I L S   A N D   I N F E R E N C E S

2 Listen to segments from the conversation again. Answer the questions during the pauses.

SEGMENT 1

1. How does the woman sound?

    a. impatient

    b. excited

    c. worried

    d. angry

SEGMENT 2

2. Besides drowsiness, what is another side effect of antihistamines?

_____

SEGMENT 3

3. What is the pharmacist concerned about?

_____

4. What does the woman need to find out?

_____

SEGMENT 4

5. How does the woman sound?

    a. surprised

    b. happy

    c. worried

    d. amused

LISTENING FOR LANGUAGE

3 Read the information about ways of expressing worry and reassurance in English.

CONVERSATION TOOLS
Expressing Worry and Reassurance

In the conversation, the pharmacist says, "...what *I'm concerned about* is you, you're having difficulty sleeping? ...if it's just occasionally then *I wouldn't worry*..."

Notice the language he uses to express his concern about using Benesec every night and then to reassure the caller that it's OK to use it occasionally. Here are other ways of expressing worry and reassurance:

Expressing worry	Reassuring
I'm (a little) worried / concerned / anxious / afraid / scared (about) / (because) ...	I wouldn't worry (if I were you).
	There's no need to worry / panic / be concerned.
	Don't worry / panic / get excited.
I'm not (real) comfortable (with) / (about)	Don't be concerned.
	(I'm sure) it's nothing serious.
	It'll be OK.

4 Listen to short conversations and fill in the blanks with the expressions you hear.

1. **Woman:** Betsy has had a fever for a couple of days. _____ that she might have an infection, or ...

   Friend: Oh, _____. Little kids get fevers all the time. They usually disappear after a day or two.

2. **Father:** What happened to you! There's a big black bruise on your face!

   Son: _____. It's not a bruise. It's paint.

3. **Student:** _____ that I'm going to fail this economics test. I just don't get this stuff.

   Roommate: _____. Professor Martin's tests aren't that hard.

4. **Woman:** _____ with that funny noise the car is making.

   Man: _____, but I'll have a mechanic take a look.

5 On the lines below, write three things that you are worried about. (If you are not worried about anything, use your imagination!)

Example:

my grade in this class

1. _____

2. _____

3. _____

Work with a partner. Tell your partner about the things on your list. Your partner should respond by reassuring you.

Example:

A: I'm worried about my grade in this class.

B: Don't worry. You're one of the best students in this class.

C. Real Talk: Use What You've Learned

VOCABULARY REVIEW: DISCUSSION

1 Find a magazine advertisement for a medication and bring it to class. Work in groups and interview each other about the medications in the ads. Take turns asking and answering the following questions; remember to use the boldfaced expressions from Part Two:

1. What is the name of the medication?

2. What medical problem is it used for?

3. Is it sold over-the-counter or by prescription?

4. What are its possible **side effects**?

5. Is it **habit forming**?

6. What are the **long-term** effects of taking this medicine?

2 Work in small groups. Discuss the questions.

1. Do you prefer to use prescription medicines or natural **remedies**, including **herbs**?

2. How do people get medicines in your country—from a pharmacy, from a **physician** or some other way?

ROLE PLAY

Role play one of the following telephone conversations with a partner. Be sure to use expressions of worry and reassurance.

1. *Roles:* A young parent and a pediatrician

   Situation: The parents are worried because their new baby cries all the time. The doctor explains that this is quite common for some babies. It is usually caused by gas in the baby's stomach. It will pass in time; they should be patient and not worry.

2. *Roles:* A pharmacist and a customer

   Situation: The customer, who suffers from headaches, has been using aspirin, but it upsets his or her stomach. The pharmacist reassures the customer that there are other painkillers (such as acetaominophen and ibuprofen) available over the counter which are safe and which do not cause this problem.

3. *Roles:* A pharmacist and a customer

   Situation: The customer has been having trouble sleeping and has been using over-the-counter sleeping pills. However, they do not work well. Also, the customer is worried that the pills could be habit forming. The pharmacist advises the customer not to worry and tells the customer to make an appointment with a doctor because there are prescription medicines that work better and are not habit forming.

Part Three: On the Air

A. Prelistening

DISCUSSION

You will hear a news report about obesity. Before you listen, discuss the following questions with a partner or in a small group.

- Which of the words in the box on the next page would you use to describe the people in the photos on the next page. Which words would you add?

  Example: The woman in the short skirt looks slim.

- What kinds of health problems might some of these people have now or in the future?

- What is obesity? Do you think it is a serious health problem? Why or why not?

fat	heavy	obese	slim	underweight
healthy	skinny	overweight	thin	

VOCABULARY PREVIEW

Read the sentences. Using the context, guess the meanings of the boldfaced words and expressions. Then match them with their definitions. You will hear this vocabulary in the news report.

1. _____ Rice is an important part of the Japanese **diet**. Most Japanese eat it every day.

2. _____ Every year, health care professionals fight to keep influenza from becoming an **epidemic**.

3. _____ Sara has had **diabetes** since childhood, so she has to be very careful about eating sweets.

4. _____ If my grandfather doesn't take medicine to lower **hypertension**, he might get a heart attack.

5. _____ By now it is a well-known fact that smoking is **linked to** lung disease.

6. _____ Students love to eat at McDonald's because the food is cheap and the **portions** are large.

---

a. serious disease in which there is too much sugar in your blood

b. high blood pressure

c. sudden spread of a disease over a large area

d. connected to or caused by another situation or fact

e. amount of food for one person

f. kind of food that someone eats each day

B. Listening

MAIN IDEAS

🎧 ① **Listen to a news report about obesity. Then answer the questions.**

1. Which of the following would be the best title for this report?

   a. Visitors to the United States Find Americans Fat

   b. World Health Organization Fights Obesity

   c. Obesity No Longer Just a U.S. Problem

2. Which of the following are included in the report? Circle the letters of correct items.

   a. statistics about obesity in the United States

   b. statistics about obesity around the world

   c. advice about losing weight

   d. definition of obesity

   e. causes of the obesity epidemic

   f. food trends around the world

   g. health problems related to obesity

DETAILS AND INFERENCES

🎧 ② **Listen to the report again. Take notes on important statistics on the increase of obesity as well as on its causes.**

🎧 ③ **Listen to the report again. Fill in the missing details.**

	United States	World
Statistics	• _____ overweight • _____ obese • _____ severely obese	• Obese adults: _____ ➤ 300 million from 1995 to 2000
Causes	• Huge variety of _____ _____ _____ • High fat / energy dense foods in _____ _____	• Diet becomes Americanized ➤ _____ • _____ children overweight

4 Work with a partner and compare answers in Exercise 3. Then take turns making sentences about the information in the chart.

Example:

Two-thirds of American adults, or 127 million people, are overweight.

LISTENING FOR LANGUAGE

5 Read the following information about reporting verbs and phrases.

CONVERSATION TOOLS

Reporting Verbs and Phrases

News reports often include the sources of facts and statistics. Sources may be experts, officials, organizations, or surveys. Note some of the verbs and phrases that connect sources and facts:

- U.S. health officials **say** . . .
- The 2000 National Health and Nutrition Examination Survey **found** that . . .
- The World Health Organization **calls** obesity an escalating global epidemic.
- The health organization **points to** the . . .

Other Common Reporting Phrases

- **According to** one study, . . .
- **X reports / notes / suggests / claims / points out that** . . .

6 Listen to the following sentences. Fill in the missing source and reporting phrase.

1. _____ in Boston _____ that the traditional Chinese martial art Tai Chi appears to have health benefits for older patients.

2. _____ from the Tokyo University Hospital, greater consumption of coffee tends to reduce the risk of adult diabetes.

3. _____ that antibacterial soaps and cleansers do not prevent disease.

4. Health risks from current genetically modified foods are very low, _____ recently published by the _____.

5. _____ done at the University of Wisconsin _____ that drinking green tea may be helpful in treating certain kinds of cancer.

7 Work with a partner. Each partner should look at one of the boxes below. Use reporting verbs and phrases to make sentences about the information in your box. Then listen to your partner's sentences and take notes on your own paper.

STUDENT A

Source	Information
World Health Organization	France, Italy—best overall health care systems
Authorities in India	1,600 cases of polio in 2000
National Women's Health Information Center	One-fifth of American women smoke

STUDENT B

Source	Information
Rand Corporation	Health care spending by obese Americans 36% higher than by normal-weight Americans
Thai government	Bird flu epidemic over
A study in China	Tea drinkers—as likely to develop cancer as non tea drinkers

C. Real Talk: Use What You've Learned

VOCABULARY REVIEW: DISCUSSION

Work in small groups. Discuss the following questions. Remember to use the boldfaced expressions from Part Three. Use reporting verbs and phrases when appropriate.

1. According to the report, what are the causes of the global **epidemic** of obesity? What other causes are there?

2. Obesity is linked to a number of physical health problems. How might obesity and being overweight be **linked to** a person's *psychological* health?

3. How does your society view (treat) overweight and obese people?

4. Look at the graph below on obesity in various countries. What trends do you notice? Compare and discuss weight problems among

   • men versus women

   • developed versus developing countries

Do you think the differences are caused by cultural or economic factors?

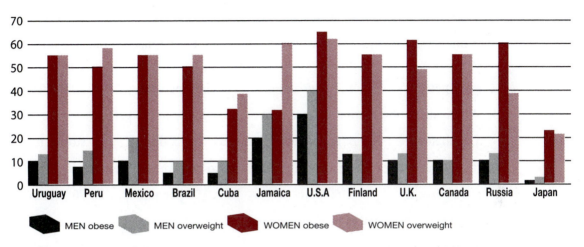

Source: Reprinted from Perspectives in Health Magazine, *the magazine of the Pan American Health Organization, published in English and Spanish.*

Part Four: In Class

A. Prelistening

DISCUSSION

You will hear a lecture about different diets. Before you listen, discuss the following questions with a partner or in a small group.

• Describe the man in the picture. How did he probably look before? Have you ever known a person who lost a lot of weight? How did the person do it?

QUIZ: OBESITY AND WEIGHT LOSS

How much do you know about being overweight and dieting? Take the quiz below and find out. When done, check your answers on page 152. How does your score compare with those of your classmates? Did any of the answers surprise you?

1. The rate of obese children has doubled in the last how many years?

   a. 20 years   b. 30 years   c. 15 years   d. 10 years

2. If one parent is obese, how much chance does a child have to become an obese adult?

   a. 80 percent   b. 70 percent   c. 40 percent   d. 50 percent

3. When you're obese, what disease are you most likely *not* to get?

   a. diabetes   b. gallbladder disease   c. heart disease   d. stomach flu

4. If you are an obese child, how likely are you to become an obese adult?

   a. 90 percent   b. 60 percent   c. 50 percent   d. 70 percent

5. What is the best way to begin losing weight?

   a. cut out all foods   b. eat only   c. reduce your   d. drink only
      that contain fat   twice a day   portions and   liquids for
                                               be active   one week

6. When dieting, how much weight should you lose per week?

   a. $1/2$–1 kilogram   b. depends on the   c. 2–3 kilograms   d. the more
      a week   type of diet and   a week   the better
                           how overweight
                           you are

7. Which of the following is *not* part of a well-balanced diet?

   a. protein   b. sugar   c. carbohydrates   d. fat

Source: Items 1–5: http://library.thinkquest.org/TQ0312847/quiz_obesity.htm

VOCABULARY PREVIEW

Read the sentences. Using the context, guess the meanings of the boldfaced words and expressions. Then match them with their definitions. You will hear this vocabulary in the lecture.

1. _____ Meals at hospitals are prepared carefully under the supervision of **nutritionists**.

2. _____ The doctor said, "After your operation, you will need to **restrict** the type of exercise you can do."

3. _____ One **drawback** of jogging is that it can damage your knees.

4. _____ He **cut down on** the number of cigarettes that he smokes from thirty to ten a day, but he still hasn't **cut back on** coffee.

5. _____ If you have a **deficiency** of vitamin C, you can get a disease called scurvy.

6. _____ Too much **cholesterol** can block the blood vessels and cause a heart attack.

7. _____ If you want to stay healthy, **eliminate** unhealthy habits, such as smoking and drinking alcohol.

8. _____ Are you calling the doctor just because you have a headache? Don't you think that's a little **extreme**?

_____

a. disadvantage

b. very unusual and severe; exaggerated

c. a trained person with special knowledge about foods and how they affect health, growth, and disease

d. limit or control

e. chemical substance found in fat, blood, and other cells in your body

f. completely get rid of something that is unnecessary or unwanted

g. reduced the number or amount

h. lack of something that is necessary

B. Listening and Note-Taking

LECTURE LANGUAGE: EXPRESSIONS OF COMPARISON AND CONTRAST

1 You are going to hear a lecture that compares and contrasts two popular diets. Study the charts of common expressions of contrast and similarity.

Contrast	Similarity
Fat is necessary for a healthy body. **On the other** hand, eating too much fat can cause health problems.	**Both** broccoli **and** oranges have a lot of vitamin C.
In contrast to young people, older people may suffer serious consequences from the flu.	Fresh fruits are rich in vitamins and minerals. **Similarly**, vegetables are a good source of nutrients.
Asthma used to be deadly. **However**, these days asthma is easily treatable.	Coughing can spread disease. **Likewise**, sneezing may make another person catch your illness.
Unlike aspirin, antibiotics need to be prescribed by a doctor.	Aspirin is **just like** Tylenol: they are both pain relievers.
While diets can be effective in the short term, they rarely result in permanent weight loss.	Food poisoning and the stomach flu **are alike**: they both cause terrible stomachaches.
A cold **differs** *from* the flu because the flu usually comes with a fever.	The South Beach Diet **resembles** The Atkins Diet, but they are not exactly the same.

2 Compare and contrast the following pairs of items. Use expressions from the chart in Exercise 1.

Example:

water—Coca-Cola

In contrast to Coca-Cola, water has no calories.

Both water *and* Coca-Cola are liquids.

1. fish—chicken
2. jogging—yoga
3. banana—apple
4. sore throat—runny nose
5. exercise—sleep
6. ice cream—steak

LECTURE ORGANIZATION: COMPARISON AND CONTRAST

3 Read the following information about taking notes on similarities and differences.

When describing two similar or contrasting items, lecturers usually organize information in one of the following two ways:

BLOCK ORGANIZATION

I. Coca-Cola
   A. Made from artificial ingredients
   B. Contains caffeine
   C. Always sweet
   D. Causes tooth decay
II. Coffee
   A. Natural—comes from a berry
   B. Contains caffeine
   C. Not sweet naturally
   D. Causes tooth discoloration but not decay

POINT-BY-POINT ORGANIZATION

		Coca-Cola	Coffee
	POINT A:		
	Ingredients	Chemical	Natural—bean
	POINT B:		
	Caffeine content	2.8 mg / ounce	15-18 mg / ounce
	POINT C:		
	Taste	Sweet	Not naturally sweet
	POINT D:		
	Effect on teeth	Sugar may decay teeth	Discoloration

TAKING NOTES

🎧 ④ Listen to the lecture. Take notes on your own paper. Then use your notes to complete the outline. Use the margin notes to help you.

intro		Q to nutritionist: Most effective diet?
		Answ:
	◯	
first type of diet		A. Low-fat diet
description		1.
advantage		2.
problems		3.
second diet		B.
differences		1. fat OK but cut down on carbs
	◯	
advantages		2.
problems		3.
		e.g., Atkins = too extreme
similarities		C.
of two diets		
conclusion		D. Advice
	◯	

REVIEWING THE LECTURE

5 Work with one or more classmates. Use your notes to discuss the following questions.

1. Which way did the lecturer present the information: block or point-by-point organization?

2. What are some similarities and differences between the low-fat and low-carb diets? Use expressions of comparison and contrast.

3. Why do most people gain back the weight they lose after dieting?

4. Which of the two diets does the nutritionist prefer?

5. What is the nutritionist's advice for long-term weight management?

C. Real Talk: Use What You've Learned

VOCABULARY REVIEW: DISCUSSION

Work with a partner or a small group. Discuss the following questions. Remember to use the Part Four vocabulary from the box.

cholesterol	drawback	nutritionist
cut down on / cut back on	eliminate	restrict
deficiency	extreme	

1. Study the food pyramids on the page 152. They illustrate the differences between the two diets described in the lecture. Which diet do you consider healthier? If you needed to go on a diet, which one would be easier for you?

2. What other ways of losing weight (besides those in the lecture) do you know? Which method has been the most effective for you or for someone you know?

3. Besides hospitals, what type of institutions might employ a **nutritionist**?

4. What unhealthy habit of yours would you like to **eliminate**?

5. Vegetarians don't eat any meat. What foods do they get their protein from? Do you think this is an **extreme** way of eating? What **deficiency** might this type of diet cause?

THE LOW-CARB FOOD PYRAMID   **THE LOW-FAT FOOD PYRAMID**

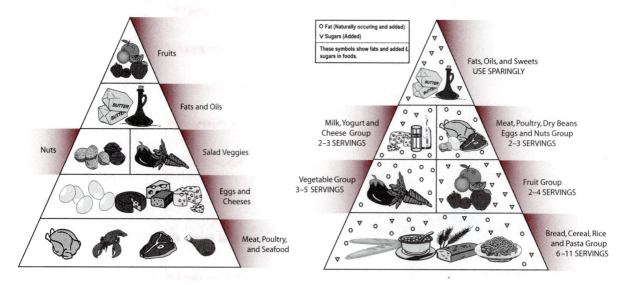

ORAL REPORT

Prepare a five-minute oral report comparing two health-related topics. Discuss their similarities and differences. Choose either block or point-by-point organization. Use expressions of comparison and contrast.

SAMPLE TOPICS

- Two types of exercise
- Two types of diets
- Two treatments of an illness (medical versus nontraditional)
- Two similar illnesses (flu versus cold)

ANSWERS TO THE OBESITY AND WEIGHT LOSS QUIZ ON PAGE 146.

1. b;   2. a;   3. d;   4. d;

5. c;   6. a;   7. b

7

Shop 'til You Drop

Part One: In Person

A. Prelistening

DISCUSSION

You will hear a conversation about a store's return policy. Before you listen, discuss the following questions with a partner or in a small group.

- Look at the picture above. What is happening?
- What is this store's rule about returning sale merchandise?
- Have you ever had a problem returning something to a store? Where? What was the problem? Who did you talk to? What did you say? What happened in the end?

VOCABULARY PREVIEW

Read the sentences. Using the context, guess the meanings of the boldfaced words and expressions. Then match them with their definitions. You will hear this vocabulary in the conversation.

1. _____ Customer: "This chair is **defective**. It broke the first time I sat in it." Store clerk: "Would you like to exchange it?"

2. _____ Most U.S. businesses have a no-smoking **policy**. If you want to smoke, you must go outside.

3. _____ Although my book report was due on Friday, my teacher **gave me a break** and let me turn it in on Monday because I was sick.

4. _____ The **headquarters** of Microsoft Corporation is in Bellevue, Washington.

5. _____ "You paid $45 for a T-shirt? What a **rip-off**!"

6. _____ A new car costs almost $40,000. We **can't afford** it. We'll have to get a used one.

7. _____ Houses in most big cities **cost a fortune**, so most people live in apartments.

8. _____ There were ten people waiting to pay, but only one **register** was open.

---

a. price that is much higher than the real value of the item (*informal*)

b. official rule of a company or organization

c. machine used in stores to calculate and record how much customers pay

d. not made correctly or not working properly

e. unable to buy something because you don't have enough money

f. (be) very expensive

g. main building or central office of a large organization

h. give someone special permission to break rules

B. Listening

MAIN IDEAS

1 Listen to a conversation between a customer and a salesclerk. Then answer the questions.

1. What is the customer's complaint? What does she want?

   _____

2. What is the store's refund policy, according to the clerk?

   _____

3. What is going to happen next?

   _____

2 Listen to a second conversation. Then answer the questions.

1. Who are the speakers?

   _____

2. At the end of the conversation, does the customer get what she wants?

   _____

Now work with a partner and compare answers.

DETAILS AND INFERENCES

3 Before listening again, try to answer the questions below.

1. The customer can't exchange the jacket because _____

   _____

2. True or False: Because the jacket was defective, the clerk offers to give the customer a store credit. _____

3. True or False: The customer did not read the store's refund policy when she bought the jacket. _____

4. True or False: If the customer had known about the refund policy, she probably wouldn't have bought the jacket. _____

5. True or False: The customer has never shopped in this store before. _____

6. True or False: The manager thinks it's a good idea for the customer to write a letter of complaint to the company headquarters. _____

7. True or False: Normally the store is too expensive for this customer. _____

8. True or False: The manager offers the customer a discount on her next purchase. _____

9. When the manager says, "My hands are tied," she means that

    a. it is not her job to give refunds.

    b. she does not have the authority to give the customer a refund.

    c. she works for a large corporation.

    d. the company policy is unfair.

Now listen to the conversations again and check your answers.

LISTENING FOR LANGUAGE

4 **Read the information about reductions.**

FOCUS ON SOUND
More Practice with Reductions

• In Chapter 3, you learned that unstressed words are often reduced in spoken English. This means that some vowels and consonants may change or disappear.

Unstressed vowels are usually reduced to schwa. The phonetic symbol for this sound is /ə/, and it is usually pronounced *uh*. You can hear a schwa in most unstressed prepositions, auxiliaries, and pronouns. For example: *to* ➤ *ta*; *for* ➤ *fer*; *you* ➤ *ya*.

• The sound *h* is usually dropped in unstressed words and syllables. For example, *get her* becomes **getter**.

• The conversations in this section contain the following reduced phrases:

Unreduced form	Reduced form
would you	*wood-ja*
did you want to	*did-ja-wan-na*
would have	*wood-uh*
couldn't you	*kood-en-cha*
give me	*gim-me*

🎧 **5** Listen to sentences with reduced forms. Write them using correct spelling.

1. _____ exchange the jacket _____?

2. _____?

3. _____.

4. _____.

5. _____ when I bought the jacket or I never

   _____.

6. _____?

6 Check your answers. Then listen again and try to repeat the sentences with the reduced forms. Remember: Reduced forms are unstressed.

7 Study the chart below to learn more idioms for talking about prices.

CONVERSATION TOOLS

Talking about Prices

The following list includes idioms from the conversations you heard and other expressions for talking about prices. Notice which expressions are noun phrases, verbs, and adjectives.

Meaning	Idioms
Too expensive	Twenty-five dollars for a T-shirt? That's a **rip-off!**
	The dress she wore at the wedding **cost a fortune**.
	Calling our daughter long distance every day is **costing** us **an arm and a leg**.
	If you only shop at fancy stores, you will end up **paying through the nose**.
Inexpensive; a good price	An excellent steak dinner at $8.99 is **a good deal**.
	I bought a used computer in good condition for $150. **What a steal!**
	Tom got **a bargain** when he bought a nice suit at half price.
A reduced price	These gloves usually cost $20, but I bought them **on sale** for $9.
	All the CDs in that store are **marked down** as much as 25 percent.

8 Practice using the idioms in Exercise 7 to talk about prices. Work with a partner. Read the item and the price to your partner. Your partner uses an idiom in a complete sentence to give an opinion.

Example:

A: A quart (liter) of milk for $3.50.

B: That's a rip-off.

STUDENT A

a. an imported silk blouse for $5

b. a 1996 Toyota with 80,000 km for $12,000

c. a sandwich for $1.59

d. a used grammar textbook for $16.50

STUDENT B

a. a package of five pencils for 15¢

b. a steak dinner for two people for $9.99

c. a pair of jeans for $99.00

d. a movie ticket for $18.00

C. Real Talk: Use What You've Learned

VOCABULARY REVIEW: DISCUSSION

Work with a partner or a small group. Discuss the following questions. Remember to use the Part One vocabulary from the box below. Try to reduce unstressed words.

can't afford	headquarters	a rip-off
cost a fortune	policy	(someone's) hands are tied
give (someone) a break	register	

1. In the conversation you heard, whose fault was it that the customer didn't know about the store's refund **policy**?

2. Do you think the manager could or should have **given** the customer **a break** and refunded her money? When a store employee tells you that something is company policy, do you believe **their hands are tied**?

3. Would you shop at a store that didn't give **refunds**?

4. Do you ever shop at the most expensive shop in your city? If not, why not?

5. In your native country, what happens if you want or need to return an item to the store where you bought it? Can you get a refund? Do stores allow you to exchange an item? Can you **get store credit**?

ROLE PLAY

1 Read the culture note before you choose a role play.

> ## Culture note: Tips for Complaining in the United States
>
> - Politely tell the clerk or customer service representative (1) what the problem is and (2) what action you want—a refund or an exchange, for example. Do not be embarrassed.
>
> - If you don't get the results you want, ask to speak to a higher-ranking employee—such as the manager or department head, or even the owner or president of the company.
>
> - If you are still dissatisfied, let the owner or head of the company know that you are going to complain to the Better Business Bureau[1] or the state or local government agency that regulates its industry.
>
> - To prevent future problems, always ask about a store's refund policy before you buy anything. And hold on to your receipt!

2 Role play one of the shopping scenarios below with a partner. One student is a customer and the other is a salesperson. If you are the customer, say what the problem is and ask for the action you want. Use vocabulary for talking about prices, page 158.

SCENARIO 1

Customer: You bought a small camera on sale. When you got home, you realized you had made a mistake—the camera does not have a zoom lens. Go back to the store and try to exchange it.

Salesperson: Help the customer exchange the camera, but tell the customer that a new one will cost $30 more because of the zoom lens and because this camera is not on sale.

---

[1] Offices of the Better Business Bureau are found all across the United States and Canada. Their purpose is to keep records of consumer complaints and to provide information about companies accused of dishonest or illegal activities. For more information, go to the BBB website at http://www.bbb.org/.

SCENARIO 2

Customer: You bought a pair of shoes. You want to return them and get a refund because they are not comfortable. Unfortunately, you have lost the receipt.

Salesperson: Without a receipt you are not able to refund the customer's money. You can only exchange the shoes or give a store credit.

SCENARIO 3

Customer: Two months ago you bought an expensive coffeemaker at a small appliance store. You've never used it, so you decide to take it back to the store and ask for a refund.

Salesperson: Explain to the customer that your store offers refunds only within thirty days of purchase. After that, customers can exchange or get a store credit. This policy is on a sign next to the cash register.

Part Two: On the Phone

A. Prelistening

You will hear a conversation about renting a car. Look at the advertisement. If you wanted to rent a car from this company, what additional information would you ask for? List your questions below:

- _____
- _____
- _____

VOCABULARY PREVIEW

Read the sentences. Using the context, guess the meanings of the boldfaced words and expressions. Then match them with their definitions. You will hear this vocabulary in the conversation.

1. _____ You have two **options** when buying a computer: Buy it in a store or buy it on the Internet.

2. _____ This hotel offers excellent service at **competitive** rates.

3. _____ They **quoted** us $800 for car repairs! I think we'll look for a cheaper repair shop.

4. _____ My passport is **valid** until 2010; then I'll have to renew it.

5. _____ This car is so small, it can only seat three people **max**.

6. _____ Ken **shopped around** until he found the suit he wanted.

7. _____ If your baggage weighs too much, you have to pay a **surcharge** on your plane ticket.

8. _____ When I bought this raincoat, I got a free umbrella as part of the store's **promotional** package.

9. _____ **As long as** you have the receipt, you can return the jacket to the store.

_____

a. tell a customer the price you will charge for a service or product

b. the maximum; the largest amount or number possible (*informal*)

c. search for the best price or item

d. money added to the regular price

e. created to advertise something

f. if; on the condition that

g. cheaper price than others but still good quality

h. officially legal, acceptable for a specific period of time

i. choices

B. Listening

MAIN IDEAS

🎧 **1** You will hear a woman shopping around for the best car rental company. Divide into two groups. Each group will hear a different phone call. Listen and take notes on a piece of paper. After listening, use your notes to answer the following questions:

1. What is the main purpose of the call?

   _____

2. Who needs to rent a car?

   _____

3. What does the caller decide at the end?

   _____

DETAILS AND INFERENCES

🎧 **2** Listen again. Fill in the chart with details about the car rental choices you heard. Remain in separate groups. Note: If a piece of information is not given, leave the box blank.

	Call 1	Call 2
	Best Deals Car Rental	**Discount Cars**
Daily rate	$39	
Weekly rate		
Mileage		
Insurance		included
Tax		
Foreign license		
How many drivers allowed		
Age limit / surcharge		
Special package		

3 Share your information with a partner from the other group. Then decide which rental company the woman should choose. Share your decision with the whole class and explain.

LISTENING FOR LANGUAGE

4 Read the following information about intonation of questions.

FOCUS ON SOUND
Intonation of Questions

In Chapter 5, you learned that:

- *Yes /no* questions end in rising intonation.
- Information (*Wh-*) questions end in falling intonation.

Two more question types are also common in English:

- Choice questions

Nonfinal choices end in rising intonation. Final choices end in falling intonation.

Example:

Do you want the <u>daily rate</u>, the <u>weekly rate</u>, or the <u>monthly rate</u>?

- Statement questions

Some statements can become questions if the speaker uses rising intonation at the end.

Example:

Statement: The daily rate is $39.   Question: The daily rate is $39?*
*This type of question is often asked when the speaker (1) is surprised or (2) wants to confirm the answer.

5 Practice the intonation patterns. Follow the steps below.

1. With a partner, take turns reading the following questions and marking your partner's intonation. Draw rising ⬈ or falling ⬊ arrows to show the direction of the intonation.

2. Listen to the questions from the two phone calls and check to see if you marked the correct intonation pattern. After you listen, practice saying the questions with a partner.

Example:

Weekend specials? And what are they?

1. How can I help you?
2. May I help you?
3. When, uh, when did you need the car?
4. Do you know what size car?

5. The—what are the different options?

6. Would you like me to reserve one for you?

7. Oh, they do?

8. And is tax included, or is that extra, too?

9. And is that OK if they don't have a local driver's license?

10. What kind of car are you interested in?

11. How many people?

12. So are we looking at a mid-size car, a mini-van, or an SUV?

13. What about per day?

14. Is that your lowest rate?

15. What's your policy about drivers under twenty-one?

16. $5 extra per day?

C. Real Talk: Use What You've Learned

VOCABULARY REVIEW: CONVERSATION

Read the conversation below. Use the Part Two vocabulary to fill in the blanks. Use the correct grammatical form.

as long as	options	quote	surcharge
competitive	promotional	shop around	valid

A: I'm thinking about buying a new computer.

B: Be sure to _____. Several stores are offering

1

_____ deals this month.

2

A: I know. One place I called _____ me a great price—just under

3

$600. But this offer is only _____ until Monday.

4

B: Hmm. Why don't you check on the Internet before you decide. Their deals are

usually even more _____.

5

A: Yes, the Internet is another good _____. But you pay a

6

_____ for shipping.

7

B: Come on. _____ their prices are low, who cares about shipping?

8

Work with a partner. Compare answers. Then practice the conversation out loud.

INFORMATION GAP

Work in pairs. Pretend that you are shopping around for a digital camera. You already have information from one store. Your partner has information from another store. Ask your partner questions to find out what the other store offers. Be sure to use a variety of questions (yes / no, *Wh-,* choice, and statement questions) with the correct intonation. Then decide together where to buy the camera: store A or store B?

Student A should look at the chart below. Student B should look at the chart on page 166.

STUDENT A

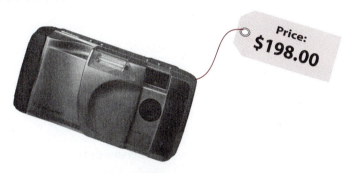

Price: **$198.00**

	Store A	Store B
Price	$198	
Tax	5%	
Shipping	Free	
Warranty	90 days	
Extended warranty	Additional 1 year: add $29	
Delivery time	8–10 business days	
Return policy	30 days with receipt and original box	
Extras	Camera case: add $24	

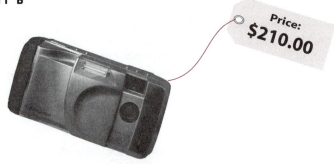

Price:
$210.00

	Store A	Store B
Price		$210
Tax		Included
Shipping		$11.95
Warranty		Ninety days
Extended warranty		Not available
Delivery time		2–3 business days
Return policy		14 days with receipt and original box
Extras		Camera case, rechargeable batteries included

Part Three: On the Air

A. Prelistening

DISCUSSION

You will hear a radio interview about types of shoppers. Before you listen, discuss the following questions with a partner or in a small group.

• In the picture to the right, what is the shopper's problem?

• When was the last time you had trouble deciding what to buy? Who or what finally helped you choose a product?

VOCABULARY PREVIEW

Read the sentences. Using the context, guess the meanings of the boldfaced words and expressions. Then match them with their definitions. You will hear this vocabulary in the interview.

1. _____ Gas, food, clothes, and other **consumer goods** are going up in price.

2. _____ A few years ago, nobody predicted the **proliferation** of digital cameras. Now almost everyone has one.

3. _____ If the goods that you buy do not **meet your standards,** the store will refund your money.

4. _____ I've never hooked up a computer to a printer, but I'm sure I can **cope with** it.

5. _____ It was a **challenge** to find shoes to match the exact color of the jacket.

6. _____ Consumerism is an **ideology** that considers buying and selling the most important activity in a society.

7. _____ I'm **plagued with doubt** about which computer to buy. Should I get a Mac or a PC? How can I decide?

---

a. be of an acceptable level of quality

b. succeed in dealing with a difficult problem or situation

c. something difficult; something that tests your ability

d. set of ideas on which a political or economic system is based

e. fast growth or increase

f. have strong feelings of uncertainty

g. products that people buy and use, especially in their daily lives

B. Listening

MAIN IDEAS

🎧 ① Listen to a radio interview with the author of a book about shopping. What are the characteristics of the two types of shoppers he describes?

SATISFIZERS

_____

_____

_____

MAXIMIZERS

_____

_____

_____

DETAILS AND INFERENCES

② Read the summary of the radio interview. Circle the words that best complete the sentences. Then listen again and check your answers.

According to Mr. Schwartz, maximizers feel that they (<u>need to / don't need to</u>)
₁
examine all the available choices. It is (<u>easy / impossible</u>) to do this. As a result,
₂
maximizers (<u>doubt / feel satisfied</u>) that they have gotten the best possible deal.
₃
On the other hand, satisfizers (<u>have / don't have</u>) reasonable standards. They
₄
(<u>are influenced by / don't care</u>) what other people think. They choose
₅
(<u>what's good enough / the best product available</u>) and (<u>worry / don't worry</u>) about
₆ ₇
the choice they've made. While shopping, satisfizers experience (<u>less / more</u>)
₈
anxiety than maximizers do. According to Mr. Schwartz, Americans assume that
some choice is (<u>good / bad</u>), and he (<u>agrees / disagrees</u>) with this ideology.
₉ ₁₀
However, he thinks that having even more choice is (<u>better / not better</u>).
₁₁

LISTENING FOR LANGUAGE

3 Read the following information about the pronunciation of the American English *t*.

FOCUS ON SOUND
The American English *t*

In North American English, *t* is sometimes pronounced as a quick *d*. This only occurs before an unstressed syllable and:

- between two vowels:

  whatever ➤ *wadever*

  digital ➤ *digidal*

- when linking words:

  way to go ➤ *wayda go*

  hit on ➤ *hidon*

- after *r*:

  thirty ➤ *thirdy*

This pronunciation of *t* is sometimes called the *flap t* and it is one of the differences between North American and British English.

4 Listen and repeat the following words and phrases from the interview. Underline the *t* where it sounds like a *d*.

1. go to buy a digital camera
2. thirty or forty different models
3. more choice is better
4. get on with their lives
5. the way to go
6. what I do
7. satisfied
8. all of the alternatives
9. Does weight matter?

5 Work in pairs. Find the differences between pictures A and B. Take turns describing the items, their locations, and the actions of the people in the pictures. Continue until you find eight differences between the two pictures. (*Hint*: Each difference involves a word spelled with *t* (or *tt*). Be sure to pronounce it correctly.)

Student A: Look at picture A only. Student B: Look at picture B only.

Example:

A: In my picture, a man is putting butter on his bread.

B: In my picture, the man is putting it back in the refrigerator because he is finished eating.

A.

B.

C. Real Talk: Use What You've Learned

VOCABULARY REVIEW: DISCUSSION

What kind of shopper are you? Take the following quiz. The vocabulary from Part Three is in boldface type. Afterward, compare and discuss your answers in small groups. Explain your answer choices. Try the American pronunciation of *t* if you feel comfortable.

QUIZ: SATISFIZER OR MAXIMIZER?

1. When shopping, I **shop around** before spending money.

   a. always

   b. sometimes

   c. never

2. I try to buy only what I really need, not what I want.

   a. always

   b. sometimes

   c. never

3. What influences your shopping choices?

   a. impulse

   b. what's being advertised at the moment

   c. my own internal standards

   d. liking the company or the brand

   e. what my friends or family buy

4. The most enjoyable way to buy things is

   a. **shopping around** carefully by going to lots of different shops.

   b. walking into one shop and buying what I want as soon as I find it.

   c. shopping online (e.g., via the Internet).

   d. using mail order.

   e. other: _____

5. How do you usually go shopping?

    a. alone

    b. with a friend / friends

    c. with my boyfriend / girlfriend

    d. with parents or other family members

6. After I buy something, I am **plagued with doubt** about the purchase.

    a. always

    b. sometimes

    c. never

7. Compared to my parents', my **ideology** about shopping is

    a. very different.

    b. very similar.

8. Based on your answers to items 1–7, do you think you are a maximizer or a satisfizer? _____

Part Four: In Class

A. Prelistening

DISCUSSION

You will hear a lecture about product placement. Before you listen, discuss the following questions with a partner or in a small group.

- The photo is from a television drama called *24*. Why do you think an Apple computer appears in the scene? How did it get there? Who benefits from placing this product in the scene?

- Can you think of other examples of name-brand products in movies, television shows, or books?

VOCABULARY PREVIEW

Read the sentences. Using the context, guess the meanings of the boldfaced words and expressions. Then match them with their definitions. You will hear this vocabulary in the lecture.

1. _____ My friend and I were quite surprised when, by **coincidence**, we wore the same dress to another friend's wedding.

2. _____ After **countless** hours of window shopping, Mr. and Mrs. Daniels finally found the perfect chairs for their dining room.

3. _____ The president made a **controversial** decision to increase the sales tax. Many supported it, but many others did not.

4. _____ When I was young, my parents made me study the piano **against my will**. As a result, I hate the piano to this day!

5. _____ The difference between these two perfumes is so **subtle** that most people can't tell the difference.

6. _____ Cigarette advertising was **banned** on U.S. television in 1965. However, it is still permitted in magazines and newspapers.

---

a. opposite of what someone wants or chooses to do

b. forbidden or made illegal

c. causing disagreement because people have strong, contrasting opinions about a subject

d. not easy to see or notice

e. surprising and unexpected situation in which two related things happen at the same time, in the same place, or to the same people

f. too many to be counted

B. Listening and Note-Taking

LECTURE LANGUAGE: PRO AND CON EXPRESSIONS

1 Read the pro and con expressions in the box.

PRO	CON
• (to be) for / in favor of / in support of (something)	• (to be) against / opposed to (something)
• to support	• to oppose
• a supporter (of something) (*noun*)	• an opponent (of something) (*noun*)

2 Work with a partner. In the sentences below, fill in the blanks with all possible expressions from the box. (Most items have more than one correct answer.) Afterward, work with another pair of students and compare answers.

1. Television advertising, in the form of commercials, is a multibillion-dollar industry in the United States. Advertisers, obviously, are the biggest _____ of television commercials.

2. For viewers, one argument _____ commercials is that the profits they bring in pay for the cost of producing television programs, so viewers can watch the shows for free.

3. Most viewers, however, are _____ commercials, saying they are stupid or boring.

4. Research shows that young children often cannot tell the difference between television programs and commercials. For this reason, many parents strongly _____ commercials.

5. If you are _____ of television commercials, there are public television stations that do not air commercials.

3 Listen to parts of the lecture. Do not take notes. Answer the questions as best you can.

1. How many arguments did you hear in favor of product placement?
2. How many arguments were against it?
3. What was the transition between the pro and con arguments?

LECTURE ORGANIZATION: PRO AND CON

④ You will hear a lecture that includes arguments for and against an issue. First, read the following example of this method of organization.

Should schoolchildren be required to wear uniforms?

PRO

1. look "professional"

2. save money

3. save time shopping & getting dressed

CON

1. boring

2. children cannot express individuality

Conclusion: There are more pros than cons, so uniforms should be required.

⑤ TAKING NOTES

Listen to the lecture. Take notes on your own paper. Then look at the outline on page 176. Use your own notes to complete the outline. Use the margin notes to help you.

	Topic:
	ex:
definition	I.
	•
	•
	II.
	A. Television
	ex: Friends - Ross eating Oreo cookie
pro	III.
	A.
con	IV.
conclusion	

REVIEWING THE LECTURE

6 Work with one or more classmates. Use your notes to discuss the following questions.

1. What is product placement?
2. In which media does product placement commonly occur? Give examples.
3. What are the arguments in favor of product placement?
4. What are the arguments against it?

C. Real Talk: Use What You've Learned

VOCABULARY REVIEW: DISCUSSION

Work as a whole class. To get an idea of how product placement works, watch a movie or TV show. Make a list of all the product placements you notice.

Movie or Show	Product Placement Example

1 After completing Exercise 1, work with a partner or a small group. Discuss the following questions. Remember to use the Part Four vocabulary from the box below.

against (someone's) will	**coincidence**	**countless**
banned	**controversial**	**subtle**

1. How many examples of product placement did you notice? Did you see none, a few, a lot, or **countless** examples?
2. Was the product placement **subtle** and realistic, or did you feel that you were watching advertisements against your will?
3. Cigarette and liquor advertisements are **banned** on American television. What kind of advertisements are banned in your country?

DEBATE

Debate the pros and cons of product placement. Divide the class into two groups, pro and con. Follow the steps below.

PREPARATION

Pro group: Prepare a list of arguments in favor of product placement. Use the form below.

Arguments in Favor of Product Placement
Makes movies realistic

Con group: Prepare a list of arguments against product placement. Use the form below.

Arguments Against Product Placement
Forces people to watch ads against their will

PRESENTATION

1 Choose two students from each group to present the pro and con sides.

2 Conduct the debate as follows:

• A speaker from the pro side presents arguments.

• A speaker from the con side presents arguments.

• The second speaker from the pro side responds to the con arguments and concludes.

• The second speaker from the con side responds and concludes.

3 The class should listen and take notes during the whole debate. Afterwards they should vote on who "won."

CHAPTER **8**

Do the Right Thing

Part One: In Person

A. Prelistening

D ISCUSSION

You will hear a conversation about cheating in school. Before you listen, discuss the following questions with a partner or in a small group.

- Look at the photo. What is happening? Is this cheating, in your opinion?
- What are some ways that students cheat?

QUIZ: WHAT IS CHEATING?

Read the statements below. Mark the statements *T* (true) or *F* (false). Then turn to page 186 to check your answers.

1. _____ You should put quotation marks (" ") around anything in your paper that you copied exactly from somewhere else.

2. _____ If you use someone else's ideas in your paper but you don't use their exact words, you don't need to say where you got the information.

3. _____ In a paper, you have to give your source if the information comes from a book but not if it comes from the Internet.

4. _____ Your teacher says Friday's history test is "open book." This means it's OK to open your book and use it during the test.

5. _____ During an open-book test, you are allowed to look at your neighbor's paper.

6. _____ You and a friend are doing science homework. She understands it. You don't. It's OK for her to explain the problem to you.

7. _____ If you don't understand the science homework, it's OK just to copy your friend's answers and turn them in.

8. _____ If a group of students does homework together, it's OK for everyone to turn in exactly the same answers.

9. _____ If you copy another person's graphics, art, or computer code, it is a kind of stealing.

Source: Adapted from ChannelOne.com, "Avoiding Plagiarism," http://www.channelone.com/school/2004/02/19/cheating_quiz/index.html

VOCABULARY PREVIEW

Read the sentences. Using the context, guess the meanings of the boldfaced words and expressions. Then match them with their definitions. You will hear this vocabulary in the conversation.

1. _____ The students were supposed to **turn in** their homework on Monday, but some of them **handed** it **in** on Tuesday.

2. _____ The boy **was tempted** to steal the candy from the store but decided not to.

3. _____ Nikki was a **straight-A** student last term, but this term she got a few Bs.

4. _____ The seriousness of the crime **determines** the level of punishment.

5. _____ Can you imagine a **scenario** where everyone is honest and nobody cheats?

6. _____ The instructor knew that the students **definitely** cheated because their answers were identical.

---

a. certainly; surely

b. affect, influence, or decide the result of something

c. situation that could possibly happen

d. receiving the highest mark in all subjects

e. want to do something even though you know you shouldn't

f. give a piece of work to a teacher or boss

B. Listening

MAIN IDEAS

1 Listen to three college friends talking about cheating. Check (✓) the topics that are included in the conversation.

_____ 1. Ways that these students have cheated

_____ 2. Ways that other students have cheated

_____ 3. University rules about cheating

_____ 4. Being tempted to cheat

_____ 5. Reasons for cheating

DETAILS AND INFERENCES

2 Listen to the conversation again. Take notes on what the speakers say about the topics below. Answer *Yes*, *No*, or *Maybe* to the questions.

Speakers	Ways of Cheating	Would Cheat?	Would Be Tempted?
Male student	1. not hand in all pages of paper, lie about it to gain more time 2. _____ _____ _____	No	Yes

(continued)

Speakers	Ways of Cheating	Would Cheat?	Would Be Tempted?
Female student 1	_____ _____		
Female student 2	2. Copy answers from a straight-A student sitting next to you		

③ Discuss your answers with a classmate. Do all three students have the same views about cheating? Who do you agree with?

LISTENING FOR LANGUAGE

④ Study the phrases for expressing disbelief in the box below.

CONVERSATION TOOLS
Expressing Disbelief

Read the following segment from the conversation:

David: No, I'm never tempted to cheat.

Ilana: *Give me a break.* Come on, you've been tempted to cheat before. None of us are perfect.

David: No, me, never.

Ilana: I think *you're pulling my leg. Come on.* Be honest with us.

To express disbelief or to question the truth, the following expressions are frequently used in informal situations:

Come on.

Give me a break.[1]

You're pulling my leg.

You're putting me on.

I don't buy it.

---

[1]Here this phrase means the speaker doesn't believe something said or done. Earlier, in Chapter 7, Part One, *giving someone a break* meant *giving someone a chance.*

5 Work with a partner. Take turns asking each other the questions below. If you don't believe your partner's answers, use an expression from the box in Exercise 4.

STUDENT A

Find out if your partner . . .

has ever cheated on an exam.

would steal food if he or she were poor and hungry.

would cheat on a TV game show to win $1 million.

has ever lied about his or her age.

STUDENT B

Find out if your partner . . .

would notify the owner of a parked car that he or she accidentally damaged.

would pay to get the correct answers on a final exam.

has ever lied about his or her weight.

would do something dishonest to help a friend.

6 Read the information about the reduced pronunciation of *would* and *wouldn't*.

FOCUS ON SOUND
Reduced Unreal Conditionals *Would* and *Wouldn't*

IN QUESTIONS

would + you = would-ja

Would you ever do it? ➤ *Would-ja* ever do it?

What would you do? ➤ What *would-ja* do?

IN NEGATIVES

would + not = woudn'

I would not be tempted. ➤ I wouldn't be tempted. ➤ I *woud-n'* be tempted.

I would not cheat. ➤ I wouldn't cheat. ➤ I *woud-n'* cheat.

(*Note:* In informal spoken English, the *t* sound in *wouldn't* is not very strong and is often dropped. To hear the difference between *would* and *wouldn't*, focus on the *n* sound.)

🎧 ⑦ Listen and complete the sentences. There may be more than one word missing in each blank.

Most people _____1_____ in order to save a life, but they

_____2_____ it to save money. What

_____3_____ do? For example, _____4_____

food if you were hungry and poor? I _____5_____ if you said

yes. But the police _____6_____ so kind. What

_____7_____ and dad do if you got arrested? They

_____8_____ help you, _____9_____? But

they _____10_____ proud of you.

C. Real Talk: Use What You've Learned

VOCABULARY REVIEW: DISCUSSION

Work with a partner or a small group. Discuss the following questions. Remember to Use the Part One vocabulary from the box below. Also remember to reduce the unreal conditionals *would* and *wouldn't*.

definitely	**scenario**	**tempted**
determines	**straight-A**	**turn in**

1. Do you think young people today are more likely to cheat than they were ten years ago?

2. Look at the results of a survey of 12,474 American high school students conducted by the Josephson Institute of Ethics. The chart shows the percentage of students in 1992 who reported doing the activities listed. Predict the results for 2002.

Report Card 1992: Ethics of American Youth		
	1992	2002
Cheating on an exam in the past year	61%	
Shoplifting	33%	
Stealing from parents	24%	
Lying to parents	83%	
Lying to teachers	69%	
Lying to save money	36% (in 2000)	
Lying to get a job	28% (in 2000)	

3. Look at the complete survey results on page 186. Were your predictions correct? Would the survey show the same trend among young people in your home country? Why or why not?

4. Have you ever done or been tempted to do any of the things in the survey?

Report Card 2002: The Ethics of American Youth		
	1992	**2002**
Cheating on an exam in the past year	61 %	74 %
Shoplifting	33 %	38 %
Stealing from parents	24 %	28 %
Lying to parents	83 %	93 %
Lying to teachers	69 %	83 %
Lying to save money	36 % (in 2000)	46 %
Lying to get a job	28 % (in 2000)	37 %

Source: http://www.josephsoninstitute.org/Survey2002/Report-Card-2002_data-tables.pdf

ANSWERS TO QUIZ ON PAGE 80

1. T   3. F   5. F   7. F   9. T
2. F   4. T   6. T   8. F

TAKE A SURVEY

Interview three English speakers about the topics in the survey in the previous exercise. Follow the steps below.

1. Change each survey item into a question. (See the first item as an example.)
2. Record the responses in the chart.
3. Share your findings with your class.
4. Tally the survey results from the whole class. Make statements using statistical expressions you learned in Chapter 1, page 24.

Example:

Forty percent of the people we asked have cheated on exams.

More than half of them have been tempted to cheat but haven't.

Ethics Survey

Number of Respondents ___3___

| | Name _____ | Name _____ | Name _____ |
	Age _____	Age _____	Age _____
Cheated on an exam in the past year Have you ever cheated on an exam?	____ Yes ____ No ____ No, but has been tempted	____ Yes ____ No ____ No, but has been tempted	____ Yes ____ No ____ No, but has been tempted
Shoplifting	____ Yes ____ No ____ No, but has been tempted	____ Yes ____ No ____ No, but has been tempted	____ Yes ____ No ____ No, but has been tempted
Stealing from parents	____ Yes ____ No ____ No, but has been tempted	____ Yes ____ No ____ No, but has been tempted	____ Yes ____ No ____ No, but has been tempted
Lying to parents	____ Yes ____ No ____ No, but has been tempted	____ Yes ____ No ____ No, but has been tempted	____ Yes ____ No ____ No, but has been tempted
Lying to teachers	____ Yes ____ No ____ No, but has been tempted	____ Yes ____ No ____ No, but has been tempted	____ Yes ____ No ____ No, but has been tempted
Lying to save money	____ Yes ____ No ____ No, but has been tempted	____ Yes ____ No ____ No, but has been tempted	____ Yes ____ No ____ No, but has been tempted
Lying to get a job	____ Yes ____ No ____ No, but has been tempted	____ Yes ____ No ____ No, but has been tempted	____ Yes ____ No ____ No, but has been tempted

Part Two: On the Phone

A. Prelistening

DISCUSSION

You will hear a conversation about a lost watch. Before you listen, discuss the following questions with a partner or in a small group.

Lost & Found

- Where was this photo taken? What are some other places where you might find a "lost and found" department?

- In your country, what do people do or where do they go if they find something in the street and want to return it to its owner?

- A well-known English saying is "Finders keepers, losers weepers." What does this saying mean? Do you have a similar saying in your language?

VOCABULARY PREVIEW

Read the sentences. Using the context, guess the meanings of the boldfaced words and expressions. Then match them with their definitions. You will hear this vocabulary in the conversation.

1. _____ When you're finished using my book, could you please **drop** it **off** in my office?

2. _____ There was a $2,000 **reward** for anyone who gave the police information about the stolen painting.

3. _____ Announcement: Will the person who lost a blue sweater please come to the information desk to **claim** it?

4. _____ If you give $100 or more to our organization, you will **be entitled to** two free tickets to any concert you choose.

5. _____ Instead of selling our old car, we **donated** it to the Red Cross.

6. _____ My favorite **charity** is the Red Cross because of the important help it gives to victims of war and natural disasters.

7. _____ I love my teacher because she always **encourages** me to do my best and never criticizes me when I make a mistake.

a. something (often money) that you receive because you have done something good, right, or helpful

b. an organization that gives money, goods, or help to people who need it

c. give something useful to an organization or person that needs help

d. say or do something to help someone have courage or confidence

e. have the right to have, receive, or do something

f. leave something at an agreed upon place

g. take something that belongs to you

B. Listening

MAIN IDEAS

1 Listen to a recorded message and the short conversation that follows. Complete the statements below. Then discuss your answers with a partner.

THE RECORDING

1. This is a recorded message from _____.

2. If you have lost something, you should _____.

3. If you find an object, you should _____.

THE CONVERSATION

1. The two speakers are _____ and

   _____.

2. The caller found _____.

3. The caller asks about a _____.

DETAILS AND INFERENCES

🎧 ② Listen again. Mark the statements *T* (true), *F* (false), or *I* (impossible to know) based on the information given. Then compare answers with a partner.

_____ 1. The police department responds to phone messages about all lost objects.

_____ 2. You should leave a message if you have lost your sunglasses.

_____ 3. It is not necessary to leave a message about found objects.

_____ 4. The university does not give out information about rewards for lost objects.

_____ 5. If no one claims the watch after 100 days, the caller can keep it.

_____ 6. The caller is going to keep the watch.

LISTENING FOR LANGUAGE

③ Review the rules about stress and linking in phrasal verbs.

FOCUS ON SOUND
Review of Stress and Linking in Phrasal Verbs

In Chapter 4, you learned several facts about phrasal verbs:

- The second word of a phrasal verb—the preposition—is stressed:

  call in

- When the second word begins with a vowel, the two words in the verb phrase are linked:

  call in

- If the direct object is a pronoun, it comes between the verb and the preposition. In many cases the entire phrase will then be linked:

  drop her off

  turn it in.[1]

---

[1] Remember to pronounce the flap *t* in linked phrases: "turn it in" ➜ turn-id-in

4 The phrasal verbs below appear in the recordings. Practice saying them with and without the pronoun *it*. Then, with a partner, make two-line conversations like the example. Concentrate on proper stress, linking, and pronunciation of the flap *t*. If you need to review the meanings of these verbs, look in a dictionary.

Example:

A: What should I do with the key I found in the library book?

B: Turn it in.

call in   drop off
give out   turn in
bring in   think over

5 Read the information about signaling imaginary situations.

CONVERSATION TOOLS
Signaling Imaginary Situations

In the conversation between the caller and the police officer, the caller asks: "What if I bring it [the watch] in and nobody claims it? Then can I keep it?"

The words *what if* signal that the speaker is imagining this scenario. Signals with the same meaning are:

(Let's) say . . .

Suppose . . .

In fact, sentences with these signals are a type of present unreal conditional. In writing and in a more formal speaking situation, the verbs would need to be in the past tense: "What if I *brought* the watch in and nobody *claimed* it?"

6 Work with a partner. Take turns using the information in your box to form questions about the situations. Use the unreal conditional. Then form a follow-up question. Your partner should answer truthfully using the unreal conditional.

Example:

Your friend didn't copy a term paper from the Internet.

A: What if your friend copied a term paper from the Internet? What would you do?

B: If my friend copied a term paper from the Internet, I wouldn't tell on him, but I would lose respect for him.

Student A

1. Your friend didn't copy a term paper from the Internet.

2. Your boyfriend / girlfriend / best friend didn't lie to you.

3. You aren't in love.

4. You didn't lose your passport

5. You have a computer.

Student B

1. Your friend didn't cheat on the final exam.

2. You can't speak six languages.

3. You didn't leave your book bag on the bus.

4. You didn't see your boyfriend / girlfriend / husband / wife drinking coffee with a man / woman you've never seen before.

5. You have a job.

C. Real Talk: Use What You've Learned

VOCABULARY REVIEW: DISCUSSION

Work in small groups. Discuss the following questions. Remember to use the boldfaced expressions from Part Two.

1. Which of the following things would you do if you found a Rolex? A diamond ring? A pair of glasses? A passport?
   - **drop** it **off** at the nearest police station
   - ask for a **reward**
   - **donate** it to a **charity**
   - turn it in, then keep it if no one **claims** it
   - keep it
   - throw it away

2. Would you ever feel that you **were entitled** to keep an object you found? Explain.

3. If your friend found a Rolex, what would you **encourage** him or her to do with it?

TALK ABOUT IT

Work in small groups. Read the information. Then discuss the questions that follow.

In December of 1995, a U.S. magazine called *Reader's Digest* did an interesting experiment. Magazine employees "lost" 120 wallets in large cities and small towns across America. Each wallet contained a name, a local address, a phone number, family pictures, notes, coupons, and $50 in cash. The magazine wanted to see who would return the wallets and who would keep them. These were the results:

	Found / Returned	Percent
Total	120 / 80	67 %
Women	60 / 43	72 %
Men	60 / 37	62 %
Teens	15 / 10	67 %
Big cities	30 / 21	70 %
Suburbs	30 / 18	60 %
Medium cities	30 / 17	56 %
Small towns	30 / 24	80 %

1. Are you surprised by the results of the experiment?
2. What would you have done if you had found one of the wallets?
3. What would you have done . . .
   - if the wallet had not contained identification?
   - if the wallet had contained ID showing it belonged to Bill Gates?
   - if the wallet had contained no money?
   - if the wallet had contained $5,000 instead of $50?
   - if you had found the wallet in your country instead of the United States?

Part Three: On the Air

A. Prelistening

DISCUSSION

You will hear a radio interview about lying. Before you listen, discuss the following questions with a partner or in a small group.

- Look at the news headline. What is this news report mainly about?
- Is it always wrong to lie, or is lying acceptable in some situations? Explain.

Everyday conversations filled with lies, study finds

June 12 AMHERST, MASS.—Lying is so common that people often don't realize they're doing it, a psychologist . . .

VOCABULARY PREVIEW

Read the sentences. Using the context, guess the meanings of the boldfaced words and expressions. Then match them with their definitions on the next page. You will hear this vocabulary in the radio interview.

1. _____ Psychologists **ran a study** to find out about teenagers' sleep habits.

2. _____ I gave the policeman **accurate** answers because I didn't want to lie to him.

3. _____ Playing the piano is one of Mika's many **accomplishments**.

4. _____ Let's not talk about **mundane** things like the weather; let's discuss something more important, like politics.

5. _____ The **mean number** of cheaters at that school is four per year.

6. _____ The child looked at me so angrily that I tried to **ingratiate myself** to her by offering candy.

7. _____ Even though Michael had no experience, he tried to **build himself up** in order to impress his new employer.

a. ordinary; uninteresting

b. average; medium

c. behave in a manner designed to make another person like you

d. make someone or something seem more special or important than he, she, or it actually is; to exaggerate

e. make or conduct research

f. achievement; something done well

g. correct and true

B. Listening

MAIN IDEAS

🎧 ① Listen to a radio interview with a psychologist who has studied how and why people lie. Take notes on the answers to the questions below.

1. Describe Dr. Feldman's experiment.

_____

_____

_____

_____

2. What were the results of Dr. Feldman's research?

_____

_____

_____

DETAILS AND INFERENCES

🎧 ② Listen again. Mark the statements *T* (true), *F* (false), or *I* (impossible to know) based on the information given. Compare and discuss your answers with a partner.

_____ 1. This study focused on lying in everyday social situations.

_____ 2. Most people lie twelve times in a ten-minute conversation.

_____ 3. The people in this study were videotaped.

_____ 4. Men lie more than women do.

_____ 5. Men and women lie for different reasons.

_____ 6. The interviewer thinks that men often lie about themselves.

_____ 7. Hundreds of people participated in Dr. Feldman's study.

LISTENING FOR LANGUAGE

③ Read the information about idioms in the box below.

CONVERSATION TOOLS
Idioms for Telling the Truth and Lying

Read the following exchange from the interview:

A: Hi. How are you?

B: I'm doing well, thanks. How are you?

A: Good. And I really *mean it*.

To *mean it* is a common idiom. Speakers use this phrase to stress that their answer is true or honest.

The following idioms are frequently used when telling the truth or lying:

Truth	Meaning	Lie	Meaning
I *swear*.	To emphasize or promise that you're telling the truth	You *made that up*.	Invented something untrue
Take my word for it.	You can be sure that what I am saying is true.	Don't *stretch the truth*.	exaggerate
I'll be frank.	To say something true that other people may not like to hear	*I think that's a bunch of baloney*. (informal)	Nonsense; not true

4 Play the "Truth or Lies" game to practice idioms. Follow the steps below.

1. Sit in small groups of three or four.

2. Take turns saying three sentences about yourself: two true statements and one lie.

3. As a group, guess which statement is a lie. To help you guess, you may ask the speaker questions. Use expressions from the box in Exercise 3.

4. When everyone has had a turn, the speaker tells the truth. The student whose lie wasn't discovered is the winner.

Example:

A: I won a tennis championship when I was fifteen years old. I spoke to a famous actor in my country. I got stuck in an elevator once.

B: You met a famous actor? I think that's a bunch of baloney!

A: No, it's true, I swear. It happened three years ago.

C: What was his name?

C. Real Talk: Use What You've Learned

VOCABULARY REVIEW: DISCUSSION

Work in small groups. Discuss the following questions. Remember to use the boldfaced expressions from Part Three. Use expressions for truth and lying when appropriate.

1. What surprised you more about Dr. Feldman's study:

   • the amount of lying that people do?

   • the differences between men and women?

2. According to Dr. Feldman, people lie for three general reasons:

   • to make other people feel better

   • to **build themselves up** and **ingratiate themselves**

   • to protect themselves

   Look at the lies below and on the next page. Mark them according to the reasons above:

   F (feel better), *B* (build yourself up), or *P* (protect yourself). Then discuss which ones you have done or would be willing to do.

   _____ a lie to a friend about his or her appearance

   _____ a lie to parents about whom you went out with

   _____ a lie on your résumé about your **accomplishments**

   _____ a lie to your boss about being sick

_____ a lie to someone about his or her medical condition

_____ a lie about a gift you received but really didn't like

3. According to research, teenagers who are most socially successful (popular) are the ones who know how to lie best. Why do you think this is true?

TAKE A SURVEY

Administer the following survey to three English speakers.

SURVEY

Question	Speaker	Yes	No
1. Your friend asks if he or she looks fat. To avoid hurt feelings, would you lie?	1		
	2		
	3		
2. A police officer pulls you over and asks, "Do you know how fast you were going?" You know you were speeding. Would you lie?	1		
	2		
	3		
3. You dropped your new camera and broke it. Would you return it to the store and lie that it had been broken before you opened the box?	1		
	2		
	3		

(continued)

Question	Speaker	Yes	No
4. Your co-worker asks you to lie to your boss about why she was absent. Would you lie to get her out of trouble?	1		
	2		
	3		
5. Would you lie to your spouse about having had a two-hour lunch with your ex-boyfriend or ex-girlfriend?	1		
	2		
	3		
6. Would you lie to your child's teacher that he was sick when he actually went to a football game with you?	1		
	2		
	3		

Use the chart below to record your findings. What percent of the respondents chose to lie in the situations below? Share the answers with your class.

	Percentage	
Question	Would Lie	Would Not Lie
1.		
2.		
3.		
4.		
5.		
6.		

Part Four: In Class

A. Prelistening

D ISCUSSION

You will hear a lecture about ethical dilemmas. Before you listen, read the passage below for an example of a dilemma. Then discuss the following questions with a partner or in a small group.

A *dilemma* is a problematic situation in which you must make a choice between two courses of action, but both of them are unsatisfactory or difficult in some way. In an *ethical dilemma,* a person is forced to make a choice that involves one's beliefs about right and wrong behavior.

Here is a famous ethical dilemma: Should a poor man, having no income and no legal way of getting any money, steal food to feed himself and his starving family? In nearly all societies it is wrong to steal. At the same time, it is wrong for a man to allow his family to die from starvation. The man must make a choice to commit one wrong action in order to avoid committing the other. What should he do?

- What do you think most people would do in the situation described above? What would you do? Why?
- Have you ever been in a situation where you had to choose between two difficult courses of action? What did you do? How did you make your choice?

V OCABULARY P REVIEW

Read the sentences. Using the context, guess the meanings of the boldfaced words and expressions. Then match them with their definitions. You will hear this vocabulary in the lecture.

1. _____ People living in a new country have to **face** many challenges.

2. _____ Children learn about right **versus** wrong behavior from their parents, teachers, and the community around them.

3. _____ My friend showed her **loyalty** to me when she didn't go to the party because I wasn't invited.

4. _____ If you knew that your company president was stealing from the company, would you **make it public** or keep quiet about it?

5. _____ Smoking may be enjoyable in the **short term,** but in the **long term** it is almost certain to make you sick.

6. _____ What is the company's **strategy** for recovering the money that it lost last year?

_____

a. feeling of strong support for a person, place, or idea

b. in the near future . . . a long time in the future

c. a planned series of actions for achieving something

d. as opposed to (used when comparing two opposing or conflicting things)

e. deal with a difficult situation

f. tell everyone something that was a secret

B. Listening and Note-Taking

LECTURE ORGANIZATION: RHETORICAL QUESTIONS

1 Read the information about rhetorical questions.

> Rhetorical questions are questions that don't require an answer from the listener. Although rhetorical questions have the same structure as other questions, they are not real questions or requests for information. The purpose of a rhetorical question is:
>
> • to introduce a topic
>
> • to get the listener's attention
>
> • to express an opinion or strong feeling
>
> Example: "Who knows what the future brings?"

🎧 ② Listen to two passages from the lecture that end in *rhetorical questions.*

Write the function of each rhetorical question. After listening, work with a partner and compare answers.

1. _____

2. _____

LECTURE LANGUAGE: DIGRESSING

③ Read the following information about digressing.

Lecturers often interrupt themselves to talk briefly about a subject that is not related to their main topic. This interruption is called a *digression.* You don't usually need to take notes on digressions. Therefore, it's useful to learn how to recognize them.

The following expressions signal digressing:

• By the way . . .
• Incidentally . . .
• That reminds me . . .
• Before I forget . . .

After digressing, speakers may use the following signals to inform listeners that they are returning to their main topic:

• Anyway . . .
• As I was saying . . .
• Going back to what I was talking about . . .

🎧 ④ Listen to part of the lecture. Listen again and answer the questions.

1. What is the main topic of the passage? _____

2. What expression does the speaker use to signal a digression? _____

3. What is the topic of the digression? _____

4. What expression does the speaker use to signal her return to the main topic?

_____

Taking Notes

5 Listen to the lecture.[1] Take notes on your own paper. Then write the outline below. Use your notes to write the main points, definitions and examples. Use the margin notes to help you.

topic	
◯	
1st type	
example	
example	
2nd type	
definition	
example	
example ◯	
3rd type	
example	
example	
example	
conclusion ◯	

---

[1] The information in this lecture is adapted from the Institute for Global Ethics publication "Building Decision Skills," Chapter 7, "Analyzing Right vs. Right Ethical Dilemmas," http://www.globalethics.org/edu/excerpts/RtVsRtParadigms.pdf

REVIEWING THE LECTURE

6 Compare notes with one or more classmates. Then use your notes to answer the following questions:

1. What was this lecture mainly about?

    _____

2. Define each type of dilemma below and give an example.

    a. truth vs. loyalty

    b. self vs. community

    c. long term vs. short term

C. Real Talk: Use What You've Learned

VOCABULARY REVIEW: DISCUSSION

1 Review the Part Four vocabulary in the box below and the strategies that follow.

face	**loyalty**	**short term**	**versus**
long term	**make public**	**strategy**	

Strategies for Resolving Ethical Dilemmas:

Imagine that someone else had to make a choice that affected you. Ask yourself:

1. How would I want people to treat me if they were the ones making the decision?
2. Which choice will benefit the greatest number of people? Or, which choice will hurt the fewest people?
3. How would a person I respect behave in the same situation?
4. Which choice "feels" right?
5. Will my choice cause any **long-term** or permanent damage?
6. In five years, will I be able to look back and see that I made the right choice?

2 Work with a partner or a small group. Examples of dilemmas are listed below. Discuss what you would you do in each situation. Use the strategies on the previous page to guide you.

- Do you keep a secret or tell someone your friend is using drugs?

- Your friend has applied for a job at your work, but you know that at her last job she often called in sick. Do you tell the person in charge of hiring?

- Your parents are willing to pay for your college tuition if you major in business. You want to major in foreign languages. Should you change majors without telling them?

- Your company is polluting, but if you **make it public** you could lose your job.

- You've won a cash prize that's meant to go to your school tuition, but your family desperately needs a car to get to and from work, pick up your younger siblings, etc. Do you spend the scholarship money taking care of your family's needs now, or do you put it away to pay for college later?

- A government is keeping taxes low in the **short term** instead of raising taxes to pay for things the country needs in the **long term**.

3 For each type of ethical dilemma below, tell your partner or group about a real dilemma you have faced. What was the dilemma, and how did you resolve it? Did you ask yourself any of the questions on page 204?

- truth versus loyalty
- self versus community
- short term versus long term

APPENDIX 1   MASTER VOCABULARY LIST

Items with an asterisk are from the Academic Word List.[1]

CHAPTER 1: WHAT'S IN A NAME?

address (v.)
ancestor
authority (a person in)*
be sick of
bunch of
can't stand
differentiate*
estimated*
explicit*
get started
go through with
    (something)
hassle
immediate family
I've got to run
knight
likely
linguist
loosen up
make sense
medieval
nickname
prospective*
reaction*
reputation
statistics*
studies (n.)
tend to
tendency
titles (of people)
unconventional*
unless
What's up?

CHAPTER 2: LET'S GET AWAY!

ahead (of time)
anxiety
at random
book (v.)
carry-on luggage
casualties
check through
confront
deadline
depart
disorder
dusk
eliminate
ended up
fare
guidelines*
hazardous
insect repellent
intense*
irrational*
lack of
lead to
messed up
nonrefundable
outbreak
pack (v.)
panic-stricken
pay through the nose
phase*
purchase*
rates
ripped off
round-trip ticket
routine (n.)
show up
stay over
symptom
therapy
trim (v.)
visibility*

CHAPTER 3: LOOKING FOR LOVE

as far as (X) goes
associated with
assume*
attachment
ballpark figure
break up with
chances are
chemistry
committed*
drive (n.)
dwindling
every single one
feel bad for
fulfilled
head over heels
    in love
hook (v.)
hormones
keep in mind
left out
match (someone) up
on the basis of
passionate
pool (of people)
pretty serious
profile (n.)
pursue*
responsible for
screen (v.)
settle down
solitude
stay out of
thirty-something
wonder about

CHAPTER 4: MUSIC TO MY EARS

anticipate*
at the door
avoid
beat (n.)
chant
chorus
come after
    (someone) (v.)
component*
crack down on
deserve
detract from
emerge*
genre
lyrics
mainstream (n.)
make out
melody
monitor* (v.)
on hold
orchestra section
phenomenon*
policy
prominent
promote*
recording industry
shrug off
significant*
sold out
soothing
sophisticated
status* symbols*
sue
tapping
threat
track (n.)
upcoming

[1]The Academic Word List was developed by Averil Coxhead at Victoria University of Wellington, New Zealand. The list contains 570 word families which were selected for their frequency and usefulness in academic discourse. For more information, see http://www.vuw.ac.nz/lals/research/awl/awlinfo.html.

CHAPTER 5: GETTING THE JOB DONE

account for
bacteria
benefits*
billing
burn bridges
client
commute
confidential
considerate/
    inconsiderate
correspondence*
courteous
deal with
disparity
diverse*
etiquette
fire
follow up
forward (v.)
incentive*
involve
janitors
lead to
multitasking
outfit (n.)
packaging
perfect (v.)
philosophical*
poised
principle
promote*
proper
punch the clock
qualifications
range*
repress
resign
résumé
reward
scrub
wage
worthwhile

CHAPTER 6: TO YOUR HEALTH

alternative*
bummed out
call in sick
cholesterol
come down with
cut back on
cut down on
deficiency
diabetes
diet (n.)
drawback
drowsiness
eliminate*
epidemic
extreme
fat
go from bad to worse
habit forming
healthy
heavy
herbs
hypertension
linked to*
long-term
nutritionist
obese
out of it
overweight
portions
prescribe
protein
remedy (n.)
restrict*
side effect
skinny
slim
thin
turn out
underweight

CHAPTER 7: SHOP 'TIL YOU DROP

against my will
as long as
banned
bargain (n.)
can't afford
challenge*
coincidence*
competitive
consumer goods
controversial*
cope with
cost a fortune
cost an arm and a leg
countless
defective
give (someone) a break
good deal
headquarters
ideology*
marked down
max*
meet (your) standards
on sale
option*
pay through the nose
plagued with doubt
policy
proliferation
promotional
quote (v.)*
register (n.)*
rip-off (n.)
shop around
subtle
surcharge
valid*
What a steal!

CHAPTER 8: DO THE RIGHT THING

accomplishment
accurate*
be entitled to
be frank
be tempted
build (yourself) up
bunch of baloney
charity
claim
definitely*
determine
donate
drop off
encourage
face (v.)
hand in
ingratiate myself
long term
loyalty
make it public
mean it
mean number
mundane
pulling my leg
reward
run a study
scenario*
short term
straight-A
strategy
stretch the truth
swear
take my word for it
turn in
versus

APPENDIX 2   COMMON ABBREVIATIONS AND SYMBOLS USED IN NOTE-TAKING

Abbreviations		Symbols	
a.m.	morning	&	and
ch.	chapter	± or ~	approximately
cm	centimeter	@	at
e.g.	example	A → B	A causes *or* leads to B
ex.	example	↓	decreasing, going down
lb	pound	$	dollars
m	meter	=	equal to, the same as (Use for all forms of *be*.)
mo.	month		
Mr.	title used for all men	♀	female
Ms.	title used for all women	↑	increasing, growing
Mrs.	title used for married women	>	larger than, more than
no.	number	−	less than, take away, minus
p. *or* pp.	page / pages	♂	male
etc.	etcetera, and so on	+	more, and
ft.	feet	≠	not the same as, different
i.e.	that is, in other words	#	number
kg	kilogram	%	percent
km	kilometer	"	same as above (repeated or used again)
pd.	paid		
p.m.	afternoon, evening	<	smaller than, less than
re	regarding or concerning	?	unclear
vs.	versus, against		
wk.	week or work		
w/	with		
w/o	without		
yr.	year		

APPENDIX 3: SAMPLE OUTLINES FOR IN-CLASS LECTURES

CHAPTER 1, PART FOUR, EXERCISE 7, PAGE 25

	III. Relationship between ♀ ed. & name change
trend	♀ go to college → keep name
statistics ○	Stats
	• 1970: — ‹1% keep name
	• 1980: — 10%
	• 1990: — 23%
	• today: — 35-50%
why ○	IV. Reasons
	1. ed. ♀ marry later →
	2. work before marriage →
	3. don't want to give up profess. identity
conclusion	V. Conc
	• Last 30 yrs: ↑ in % of US ♀ college grads
○	↑ in # of ♀ who keep name
	• Total who keep name = 10%
	• Will ↑

introduction		Common phobia: Fear of flying
		Focus on treatment
	○	
definition of phobia		Phobia: intense, irrational fear
		Fear of flying — unrealistic but common
details / statistics about fear of flying		• plane travel = 20 x safer than car travel
		• yet 25 mil. Americans have aerophobia
what can help?		Treatment: behavior therapy — "desensitization" to make you less sensitive
		In therapist's office
		Phase 1: progressive relaxation
		relax muscles → control body →
	○	eliminate anxiety
		Phase 2: make list of frightening situations, rating anxiety levels
		Phase 3: imagine each situation and relax
		In the real world (phase 4): experience situations in real life — actually do things on list
		1st day: take friend to airport, go home
		2nd day: go to airport, walk in
		3rd day: go to airport, go through metal detector
		use relaxation technique to feel
		comfortable
conclusion	○	Conc:
		Total treatment = 2 mos.
		Desens. cured Harry's phobia

introduction	I. Topic: The biology of love
	Love = bio process
stages	II. Dr. Helen Fisher (Rutgers U.): love →
	3 stages w/diff. chemicals active in brain
1st stage	A. Lust
definition	1. powerful sexual attract. to another person
hormone	2. hormone = testosterone
	a. not just male hormone
	b. → sex drive in men & women
2nd stage	B. Romantic love
characteristics	1. become emotionally attached
	2. feel passionate, romantic, madly in love
hormone	3. brain chemical = dopamine
research study	4. study @ U. of London
1st step	a. volunteers saw pics of lovers
2nd step	b. saw pics of friends
	c. sci. used MRI to record brain activ.
results	5. when vol. saw pic. of lovers → part of brain that
	makes dopamine (pleasure hormone) very active
	when pic. of friends → no activity
conclusion	6. conc.: dopamine essential for romantic phase
	of love

(continued)

3rd stage		C. Attachment phase
characteristics		1. people settle down, have children
	○	2. feelings = peace, security, stability
hormone		3. important hormone = oxytocin
animal research		a. animals that rec'd it attached quickly to
		partners
		b. if hormone blocked → showed no interest
humans	○	c. humans: found in blood of men & women in
		stable relationships
role of oxytocin		4. scientists think oxy. may play imp. role in ability
		to form close relat.
	○	III. Real organ of love: brain not heart
conclusion		Love = bio. process like eating, etc.

introduction	Topic: Rap
	Why easy to recognize? Distinctive characteristics
definition **(2 components)**	Rap: genre of music
	2 components
	• rhyming lyrics
	• musical backgr./accompaniment
origins of rap	1970s: –started in NYC by young, poor Afr. Americans
	–used turntable
	–unique element: "scratching" (= unusual sound
	by moving record w/hand on turntable)
	Musical elements today:
	more sophisticated
	1. background melody (tune) can sing, can create
	w/any instrument
	2. backbeat (most prominent) (rhythm)
	repetitive drum sound
	3. sampling = take piece of recording + use in new
	recording, e.g. Coolio's song used classical recording

(continued)

other components of rap		Lyrics:
		1. gangsta rap
	◯	-early '80s
		-form of protest, frustration at difficulties,
		realities of life (drugs, gangs, guns, violence)
		-shocking language, speak about women in neg. way
		2. soft-core
		-mid-90s
		-less violent
		-still emphasized money, cars, jewelry
	◯	
		These days:
		-lyrics → more positive messages
		-rap → mainstream, e.g.:
		• rap artists in movies
		• co's use rap to sell products
		• France: rap = officially "art"; 2nd
		largest market for rap
		• fans from all races, countries
	◯	
conclusion		Conc: Rap brings people together; powerful like rock

topic	Why Amer. work hard?
intro	–Amer. work as many hrs. as Jap. + Kor.
	– " " 300–400 hrs./yr. > than West. Euro
	– take fewer vacations
	– retire later
	Reasons
	1. Historical: Euros. who settled U.S. = relig. Christians
	believed in value of hard work
	that value → until today
	2. Main reason: economic
	U.S.: wide range of sal.
	e.g.: Pres. of U.S. co. earns 50–100 x av. wkr. →
	incentives to work harder, i.e., work hard → higher pay
	Europe: wage gap smaller → less incentive
	3. To keep job w/ benefits
	benefits = med. insurance, unemp. ins., retirement
	Europe: gov. pays ben.—if people lose job
	U.S.: employer pays ben. if lose job → lose ben.
	4. Technology → people work harder
	– how? e-mail, voicemail, etc. → easier to stay in
	touch w/ office
	– good jobs hard to find → people feel pressured
positive reason	5. They enjoy working
	work gives identity, e.g. "bus-driver, teacher"
	+ sense of accomplishment
	feel part of team = Amer. value work
	work gives reward > money
summary	People work hard for reward, or out of necessity

intro		Q to nutritionist: Most effective diet?
		Answ: # of overweight people ↑, → many kinds of diets
	◯	(most = fads)
		2 common diets: low-fat, low-carb
first type of diet		A. Low-fat diet
description		1. limit fat, oils (no meat, cheese, butter, fried foods)
advantage		2. adv: low cholesterol → no ♥ disease
problems		3. disadv: bored, hungry → overeat sugary foods →
		gain back weight
second diet		B. Low-Carb diet
differences		1. fat OK but cut down on carbs (sweets,
	◯	bread, rice, potatoes); Atkins: no fruit
advantages		2. adv: lose weight
problems		3. disadv: bad for body (vitamin defic., kidney
		problems)
		e.g., Atkins = too extreme
similarities of two diets		C. Both limit food choice → hard to continue →
		gain weight back
conclusion		D. Advice
		1. eat balanced diet (all food grps)
	◯	2. reduce calories (smaller portions)
		3. exercise

Chapter 7, Part Four, Exercise 5, page 176

	Topic: product placement
	ex: Apple computer in <u>24</u>
definition	I. Def. of product placement
	• mentioning, using, showing a brand-name product as part of story
	• not commercial, but = type of advert.
	II. Media
	A. television
	ex: <u>Friends</u> - Ross eating Oreo cookie
	B. movies
	ex. James Bond - BMW, Coke/Pepsi
	C. video games
	D. pop songs
	E. books
	ex. candy in children's book
pro	III. Pro
	A. for advertisers: sells products
	ex. candy sales, after movie ET, Tom Cruise
	+ Ray Ban sunglasses
	B. for consumers: makes stories realistic
con	IV. Con
	A. expose us to adv. against our will
	B. subtle → don't realize we're seeing adv.
	C. esp. true for children (Lancaster study)
conclusion	Conc: Consumer groups want laws to restrict/ban prod. place.
	in media for kids

topic		Ethical dilemma: choice about right v. wrong behav.
		Topic: 3 types of right vs. right dilemmas:
1st type		1. Truth vs. loyalty
example		• e.g. friend using drugs - keep secret or tell?
example		• e.g. friend's dress unattractive/unprof.
		tell truth or keep quiet?
2nd type		2. Self vs. community
definition		• Def: needs of 1 person vs. needs of group/
		community
example		• e.g. parents want you to be doctor; you want
		to be artist.
		whom to please?
example		• e.g. co. or gov. spilling dangerous chemicals;
		report them or not? protect your job or
		community?
3rd type		3. Short term vs. Long term goals
example		• e.g. eat all candy now or save some
		for later (age 7)
example		• e.g. spend $ now on car or save $ for college
		(age 16)
example		• e.g. gov. keep taxes low + be pop.
		or raise taxes for new univ. 5 yrs. later?
		Conflict: needs/desires of present vs. future
conclusion		Conc:
		• Ethical dilemmas not easy
		• Useful strategies/guidelines to help make right
		choices—next topic

AUDIOSCRIPT

CHAPTER ONE: WHAT'S IN A NAME?

Part One: In Person
Page 3, B. Listening

Exercise 1

Ben: Hey, Alia.

Alia: Hey, Ben. What's up?

B: Hey, guess what? I recently met another person with a name just like yours. It sounds the same; I'm not sure if they spell it the same way, but it made me question—what does your name mean?

A: Oh, she must be Lebanese, too, because it's a Lebanese name. . . . Um, it's the Arabic word for um "high" or "lofty," so it means you're kind of above it all, looking down at things, and trying to take care of things down in . . . and kind of trying to take care of people. But that's not why I was named that. Um, I was named that because my mother loved this love story called *Alia and Assam*. And um she had me first, and then thirteen months later she had my brother, and she just loved this story, *Alia and Assam*, which is basically the Arabic *Romeo and Juliet*. So she named him Assam.

B: So did you say that your brother is thirteen minutes younger than you?

A: No, thirteen months.

B: OK, that makes more sense. And what about your last name, Alia? "Yunis" is your last name?

A: Um, yeah.

B: What does that mean?

A: It's a super-common name in Arabic. In English, it literally means "Jonah." Uh, Jonah who got swallowed by the whale in the Bible?

B: Oh, yeah. I know that story.

A: Oh, yeah. What about you? What about "Ben"? Is that your nickname, or um is your real name "Benjamin"?

B: Yes, my real name is "Benjamin." So my nickname is "Ben."

A: Yeah.

B: Um, everyone's called me "Ben" since I was a kid, so . . . I prefer "Ben" to "Benjamin." "Benjamin" sounds too formal for me.

A: Yeah, I don't . . . you don't look like a Benjamin to me; you look like a Ben. Uh, but your last name is different. "Eisenbise" is very unusual.

B: Yes.

A: You're the only Eisenbise I know.

B: I'm the only Eisenbise that I know also. It's very unusual. I've never met another person with my last name. Outside of my immediate family, of course.

A: Well, it's a German name?

B: Yeah, it's German and it means "iron bite."

A: "Iron bite"? I don't understand.

B: Uh, yeah. That's been a common reaction throughout my life. Uh, but, I lived most of my life without knowing what the meaning of "iron bite" was. Um and turns out, recently I found out—uh—that the story is from medieval times, and apparently my ancestors were Bavarian knights. . . .

A: Oh, cool.

B: Yeah, isn't that cool? And these knights taunted their opponents by holding swords in their teeth.

A: That's gross.

B: Pretty strange, yeah.

A: Yeah.

B: Yeah, and I've seen the—uh—the family shield with a picture of two knights with the swords coming out of their mouths and . . .

A: Really?

B: Yeah.

A: Where, you saw it on the Internet, or . . .

B: Yes, exactly, on the Internet, where else? I think I wouldn't have found out that information without the Internet.

Page 3, Exercise 3. Repeat the recording from Exercise 1.

Page 5, Exercise 4

Ben: So did you say that your brother is thirteen minutes younger than you?

Alia: No, thirteen months.

B: OK, that makes more sense. And what about your last name, Alia? "Yunis" is your last name?

A: Um, yeah.

B: What does that mean?

A: It's a super-common name in Arabic. In English, it literally means "Jonah." Uh, Jonah who got swallowed by the whale in the Bible?

B: Oh, yeah. I know that story.

Page 5, Exercise 5. Repeat the recording from Exercise 4.

Part Two: On the Phone

Page 9, B. Listening

Exercise 1

Judy: Hello?

Reka: Judy?

J: Yes.

R: Hi, it's Reka.

J: Hi! How are you? I haven't seen you in a long time.

R: Yeah, yeah, well. . .

J: What's happening with you?

R: You know, the usual; working hard and all that.

J: Yeah, I know, I know. So what's up?

R: Well, um, there's a question that I've been meaning to ask you for a while. Um, I remember that you changed your name a few years ago, after your divorce . . .

J: Yeah. . .

R: Right.

J: Yeah. . .

R: And um. . . I—I wanted to know how you did it. I mean legally, you know, how you changed your name legally.

J: Oh. Um, gee, that was three years ago already. OK. Well, all I remember is that I had to go downtown and fill out a bunch of forms.

R: Where downtown? In City Hall?

J: I think it was the courthouse.

R: Aha.

J: Yeah, that's it. The courthouse.

R: OK.

J: It was kind of a hassle and um I don't remember what it cost. Probably not very much. Um, why do you want to know? Are you changing your name?

R: Well, you know the business that I've been thinking about starting.

J: Yeah, the public relations thing? Are you going to do it?

R: You know, I think I'm really going to do it. I want to get started on that. I am. . . I'm so sick of working for a big company, and I think . . .

J: Hmmm.

R: I'm ready to, to stay home, work out of my house, and do my own consulting business.

J: Wow, really. Huh.

R: But. . . but here's the thing, don't laugh, OK?

J: OK.

R: I really can't stand my last name!

J: Really?

R: Yes. Yes. I've always hated it. It's too long, and people are always mispronouncing it.

J: You never told me that!

R: Yeah, yeah, and so um I want to just start with something new, you know, a new company, a new name, and a new start, you know. . . .

J: Yeah, that makes sense. Um, so have you decided the name you want to change it to?

R: Yeah, but, uh. . .

J: So?

R: I'm not ready to tell anybody yet.

J: Oh.

R: I really have to decide if I'm going to go through with it.

J: OK. Well, good luck. Let me know what you decide.

R: Of course. Of course.

J: OK.

R: So, um, thanks for the information. Um, I've got to run, and you know I'll call you soon and we'll have lunch, OK?

J: Sure, no problem. Great. I'll talk to you soon, Reka.

R: OK. Bye.

J: OK. Bye-bye.

Page 10, Exercise 2. Repeat the recording from Exercise 1.

Page 11, Exercise 4

1. I don't remember what it cost. . .
2. Probably not very much. . .
3. Don't laugh, OK, I really can't stand my last name!
4. You never told me that!
5. I'm not ready to tell anybody yet.
6. Sure, no problem. Great. I'll talk to you soon, Reka.

Part Three: On the Air

Page 16, B. Listening

Exercise 1

Avi Arditti: I'm Avi Arditti with Rosanne Skirble.

This week on Wordmaster—what to do when there's only one "you."

Rosanne Skirble: We're talking about forms of address. Speakers of other languages may be used to having two ways to address someone—one formal, the other informal. In Spanish, for instance, there's the formal "usted" and the casual "tu." But in English it's "you" and only "you."

AA: So, you may ask yourself, does that mean English speakers have no way to differentiate between formal and informal situations? We asked this question to our friend Mary Newton Bruder, the linguist better known as Grammar Lady.

Mary Newton Bruder: We do it by using people's names. So if we want to be very formal with somebody that we've just met, we use a title plus last name. So "Dr. Snow" or "Mrs. Jones" or "Miss Scafe," for example. But if we wanted to be less formal and we know the people better, then we use their first names.

AA: OK, let's say you've just met a person. Rosanne had this question for Grammar Lady: What happens when it's a situation where it's not immediately clear how formal you should be?

RS: The reason I'm asking is because we have a young man living with us this summer, who is from Atlanta; he's a college student. And, um, he calls me "ma'am." So, uh, that's something I'm not really used to.

Bruder: And he would probably call—does he call your husband "sir"?

RS: Uh-huh.

Bruder: OK, I think Southerners tend to be more formal. And you will. . . He'll probably have to be there quite a long time before he'll call you by your first name.

RS: Is this generally a big problem for people coming in from other cultures because indeed they do in their languages have these two levels?

Bruder: Well, I think it is a problem because the rules are not necessarily explicit. People will not say to a non-native or non-English speaker, "Don't call me Mary, call me Dr. Bruder," for example. I would never say that. I would never correct someone even though I felt uncomfortable by the use of my first name. I still wouldn't ever correct them.

AA: And I guess one thing you never use as a form of address is to call someone "mizz." You never say that, "Excuse me, mizz." You'd say "miss."

Bruder: And you wouldn't say "missus" either.

RS: Right.

Bruder: You would say "miss" or "ma'am."

AA: So I suppose you know people, they've come over, they're meeting with a prospective employer or a prospective school, university, that they want to attend, your advice is to be formal, but if the other person, the person in authority, suggests that you loosen up, then you should.

Bruder: Then you should do that, yes.

AA: But still refer to the person by last name, mister or miss or doctor or professor.

Bruder: Yes, unless specifically invited on more than one occasion, I would continue to use title, last name, continue to be formal for quite awhile.

Page 16, Exercise 3

AA: Rosanne had this question for the Grammar Lady: What happens when it's a situation where it's not immediately clear how formal you should be?

RS: The reason I'm asking is because we have a young man living with us this summer, who is from Atlanta; he's a college student. And, um, he calls me "ma'am." And that's something I'm not really used to.

Bruder: And he would probably call—does he call your husband "sir"?

RS: Uh-huh.

Bruder: OK, I think Southerners tend to be more formal. And you will . . . He'll probably have to be there quite a long time before he'll call you by your first name.

Page 17, Exercise 6

1. Thank you so much for the present, Miss Taylor.
2. Ms. Evans had to cancel her appointment.
3. Is Miss Adams working today?
4. I'd like to speak to Mrs. Smith, please.
5. Do you know if Mr. Rodriguez is married?
6. Do you know if Ms. Rodriguez is married?

Part Four: In Class

Page 22, Pretest

Exercise 1

Part 1 of the lecture

Lecturer: Today we're going to examine the growing trend among American women who decide not to change their family names when they get married. That is, they choose to keep their birth or maiden names even after they get married. Now you may know there are some countries, such as Korea and Saudi Arabia, where women always keep their own names at the time of marriage. But in the U.S., traditionally, women have tended to adopt their husbands' names when they got married. So, for example, Mary Smith would marry John Brown; and then she would become Mrs. John Brown.

This custom began to change only about thirty years ago. In fact, the 1970s and 1980s were a time of great change—both socially and economically. Let's look at what some of those changes were and then see how these changes influenced a woman's decision to either keep or change her name when she got married.

First of all, in the 1970s, American society began to be more open and more accepting of people who were different; people who made untraditional or nonconventional lifestyle choices. So, what did this mean for women? Well for women, unconventional or nontraditional lifestyle meant that it was more acceptable for women to go to college and have a career instead of getting married right after high school, which was the general tradition before the 1970s.

Let's look at some statistics about women college graduates:

- In 1970, 8.2 percent of American women graduated from college.
- In 1980, the percentage had increased to 13.6.

- In 1990 this percentage of women. . . American women who graduated from college was 18.4 percent.
- And in 2000, 23.6 percent of American women graduated from college.

So you see, this trend toward higher education for women, which began 30 years ago, continues to this day.

Part 2 of the lecture

Lecturer: Now, what is the relationship between a woman's level of education and her decision to keep her own last name? Do you know the answer? Well, it's quite simple. Women who go to college are more likely, much more likely, to keep their own last names than women who do not. And this trend has been growing for the last thirty years. According to several studies that have been done on this subject, in 1970 less than 1 percent of college graduate women kept their last names at the time of marriage. By 1980 this had become 10 percent. There was a huge jump in 1990 to about 23 percent. And today, it's um, it's estimated that between 35 and 50 percent of educated women keep their own names when they get married.

Now why is that? I mean, why are educated women more likely to keep their own names? The answer is that women who stay in school longer also tend to get married later. They spend a few years working before getting married and having a family. During these years they often establish a professional identity and a reputation—they kind of "make a name" for themselves—and become comfortable with their own identity— the identity or name that everyone knows them by. So, as a result, many of these women have no desire to give up this independent identity even after they get married.

So, to summarize we can see that over the past thirty years there has been a huge increase in the percentage of American women who graduate from college. And during the same time, time period, there's been a growing tendency among these educated women to keep their names when they get married. I should point out that among the entire population of American women,—I mean the population including <u>all</u> women, educated and not educated—the percentage of women who keep their own names is small—only about 10 percent. So compare 10 percent of women in general to 35 percent of college-educated women. It's a big difference, but I predict that this number will increase. As more and more women go to college, and as we see more and more women in politics, the arts, and entertainment using their own names, I expect that greater numbers of American women will make the choice to keep their maiden names when they get married.

Page 24, B. Listening and Note-Taking. Exercise 3. Listen to Part 1 of the lecture again.

Page 25, Exercise 5

Example: In 1970, only 8.2 percent of American women graduated from college.

1. By 1980, 20.9 percent of American men had graduated from college.
2. By the year 2000, the percentage of American men who graduated from college had increased to 27.8.
3. In the year 2000, 98 percent of American public schools were connected to the Internet.
4. It's estimated that there are more than 88,000 different last names in the United States.
5. In China, the number of last names is less than 400.

Page 25, Exercise 7. Listen to Part 2 of the lecture again.

Chapter Two: Let's Get Away!

Part One: In Person

Page 30, B. Listening

Exercise 1

Speaker 1: One thing that I just really can't stand about traveling, when I travel with a group of people, is uh, when somebody is late when we have a place that we're going to meet and we've agreed upon a time, and let's say we all wanted to do our own thing at some part of the day, and we want to meet back at, for dinner or something like that. Then, um, if one person's late then the whole group has to wait, and it's really inconvenient, especially when, you know when you're traveling you're in a hurry, and you want to see as much as you can in as short a time as possible. And anything that you have to wait for is really . . . it's terrible.

Speaker 2: Let's see, . . . my pet peeve when I travel . . . Well one of my pet peeves when I travel overseas is when I really need money but I can't find an ATM that takes my card, or else I finally find a machine and it's broken. So then I don't have any choice, I have to pay through the nose to change money at my hotel. It's really irritating because I know I could get a better rate at the ATM, so I end up feeling really ripped off and . . . well, irritated.

Speaker 3: Well, I travel frequently by airplane, but I take mini-vacations, so I always have just carry-on luggage; I never like to check anything through. Since 9/11, I found that it is impossible for me to carry my scissors in my carry-on luggage. Now this is a pet peeve, this really ticks me off, because I have a beard. So when I travel, let's say to Puerto Rico for a week, weekend, a long weekend, and I want to trim my mustache, I have to buy scissors in San Juan. So I trim my mustache and then of course when I go back

to New York, when I'm with my carry-on luggage, I have to leave the scissors back in my hotel room in San Juan. So I'm constantly buying scissors every time I travel. That by far is the biggest pet peeve I have.

Speaker 4: Well, one of my pet peeves about traveling has to do with what happens when you spend a lot of time packing, and then you show up at the airport. I have a routine for packing where I put certain things on the right, certain things on the left, it's all folded, it always fits perfectly. And then you go to the airport, and you get picked out of line for one of the random searches, and they unzip your duffel bag, and they go through everything. And of course they take out everything that you spent so much time putting in place so carefully so that it would look so good, um, and when they're done, nothing fits, nothing's folded the same way, uh nothing lies as flat uh as it did, and it's impossible to zip the bag down. And then when you get home, or when you get to where you're traveling, uh everything is all wrinkled and messed up and not where you put that. I hate that.

Page 30, Exercise 2. Repeat the recording from Exercise 1.

Page 31, Exercise 4

Example: it's all folded

1. can't stand about traveling
2. a group of people
3. part of the day
4. in a hurry
5. travel overseas
6. find an ATM
7. when I travel
8. spend a lot of time
9. take out everything
10. it's impossible

Page 31, Exercise 5

1. I end up feeling really ripped off and . . . well, irritated.
2. It is impossible for me to carry my scissors.
3. You get picked out of line for one of the random searches.
4. They take out everything that you spent so much time putting in place so carefully.
5. Everything is all wrinkled and messed up.

Page 32, Exercise 7. Repeat the recording from Exercise 1.

Part Two: On the Phone

Page 35, B. Listening

Exercise 1

Agent: ABC Travel Center. Mark speaking.

Customer: Uh, yes, uh, I'm calling about your rates from L.A. to New York, uh. . . I'd like to. . .

A: On what day?

C: On September 8th.

A: OK. Los Angeles to New York. Are you flying to JFK, La Guardia, or Newark?

C: JFK.

A: How many in your party?

C: Sorry?

A: How many . . . are . . . traveling?

C: Just one. Myself.

A: OK. What time do you want to leave Los Angeles?

C: I'd like to leave in the morning. Not too early, though.

A: OK. I have 7:00, 8:00, 11:25.

C: 11:25 would be fine.

A: And your return date?

C: The return date would be the 12th.

A: September the 12th. And what time did you want to leave JFK?

C: Mid-afternoon.

A: So like departing around like 1:00 or 2:00?

C: Right.

A: OK. I got a 12:00 noon or 4:15 departure.

C: OK. 4:15 would be better.

A: OK. This is on United Airlines. Round trip fare is . . . ooh, you're not . . . uh, let's see, what's the . . . that's the 8th of September . . . and you're not staying a Saturday night.

C: I could if it saves money.

A: Well, I'm going to give you prices on both, if you stay over and if you don't. If you don't stay over Saturday night, you're looking at 1,623 dollars and 68 cents. Yeah, well, now if you do stay over Saturday night, coming back on the 13th of September, the rate will be, let's see, . . . can you hang on a second?

C: Uh-hm.

A: Um, Thanks for holding. Uh, just let me check here. Brings it down to 379 dollars and 37 cents.

C: Oh, my goodness!

A: So you can see the difference. . .

C: Yeah. That's a big difference.

A: Yeah. These fares are based on today's rate. And the reason I say that's cause the rates change sometimes, uh, most of the time daily, and sometimes hourly. And this fare is a non-refundable fare. There is a 75 dollar fee for any changes once the tickets are issued, plus any increase in the fare.

C: I understand. OK, and um, when do I have to purchase this ticket?

A: OK. Now, if you made the reservation today, ticketing deadline would be within twenty-four hours. So you would have until tomorrow. That doesn't guarantee the fare.

C: Hmm.

A: We can only guarantee the fare today. But, usually it holds for twenty-four hours.

C: OK, so I'd have to purchase it in twenty-four hours. OK. Um, fine. I'd like you to book me then. And then I'll make the decision within twenty-four hours.

Page 36, Exercise 2. Repeat the recording from Exercise 1.

Page 36, Exercise 3.

1. If you don't stay over Saturday night, you're looking at 1,623 dollars and 68 cents.

2. I could if it saves money.

3. There's a 75 dollar fee for any changes once the tickets are issued.

4. So I'd have to purchase it in twenty-four hours.

5. I got a 12 noon or 4:15 departure.

6. Can you hang on a second?

Part Three: On the Air

Page 40, B. Listening

Exercise 2

1. Nearly one hundred mountain climbers have died in accidents in the Alps since the end of June, prompting Italian, French, and Swiss officials this week to issue new guidelines for climbers. While the overall number of casualties is not higher than in past years, more deaths involved groups of climbers. Officials urged groups to take along professional guides rather than reaching for glory by themselves.

2. Cover up and use insect repellent if you're in Florida–that's the advice of state health officials who warned this week of the possibility of an outbreak of deadly encephalitis. Mosquitoes carrying the disease have been found in eight Florida counties. In 1990, eleven people died during an encephalitis outbreak in the state. Health officials recommend staying covered–or even indoors–from dusk to dawn, when mosquitoes are most active.

3. It may be smog from millions of acres of burning forests in Indonesia that led to the worst airline crash in that country's history this week. More than 200 people died when an Indonesian jet crashed in the Sumatra region of the country. Pollution from those burning forests also led the government of Malaysia to declare a state of emergency, and some airports have been closed due to poor visibility. The State Department warns Americans that pollution in the region has reached hazardous levels.

4. A real worry for travelers to Tokyo this month is a lack of hotel rooms. There are only 16,000 rooms within a thirty-minute drive of Nagano. With 2 million visitors expected to attend the Olympic Games, many will take the bullet train there from hotels in the Tokyo area. If you need to stay overnight in or around Tokyo, book ahead.

Page 40, Exercise 3. Repeat the recording from Exercise 2.

Page 42, Exercise 5

1. Officials urged groups to take along professional guides rather than reaching for glory by themselves.

2. Cover up and use insect repellant if you're in Florida–that's the advice of state health officials who warned this week of the possibility of an outbreak of deadly encephalitis.

3. Health officials recommend staying covered– or even indoors–from dusk to dawn, when mosquitoes are most active.

4. Singapore radio has been urging the elderly and people with respiratory problems to stay indoors.

5. If you need to stay overnight in or around Tokyo, book ahead.

Part Four: In Class

Page 46, B. Listening and Note-Taking

Exercise 2

Lecturer: OK, so, so far in this course we've looked at a number of mental disorders, specifically phobias, and today I want to focus on one of them . . . on one of the most common phobias, the fear of flying. I'm not going to go into the causes and symptoms at this point; instead, I'd just like to concentrate on treatment. A very common treatment that is often applied to other forms of phobias as well.

Page 47, Exercise 4

Example: One definition of therapy is the treatment of an illness over a long period of time, without the use of medicine.

1. The word panic can be defined as a sudden, uncontrollable fear; a fear that causes great confusion and a strong desire to escape.

2. Let me define psychiatry. Psychiatry is a branch of medicine. It is the study and treatment of mental illness . . . uh . . . the medical treatment of mental illness.

3. Psychology is different from psychiatry. By psychology, we mean the study of the mind and the treatment of behavior disorders, uh, behavior problems.

4. Have you ever heard someone call another person psycho? As in, "that guy is a complete psycho"? In this case, the word psycho refers to a mentally disturbed, mentally sick person. But psycho is a slang word with a strong negative meaning. It's an insulting term for someone who you think is crazy or acting crazy.

Page 47, Exercise 5

Lecturer: OK, so, so far in this course we've looked at a number of mental disorders, specifically phobias, and today I want to focus on one of them . . . on one of the most common phobias, the fear of flying. I'm not going to go into the causes and symptoms at this point; instead, I'd just like to concentrate on treatment. A very common treatment that is often applied to other forms of phobias as well.

But first, let me repeat the definition of phobia that I gave you earlier. A phobia is an intense and irrational fear of things or situations. Again, the key words are intense and irrational. People who suffer from phobias know

that their fears are silly or unrealistic. For instance, people who have a fear of flying know and understand that flying is actually one of the safest forms of public transportation—that traveling by airplane is more than twenty times safer than traveling by car. But even with this knowledge, they are so terrified of flying that they're unable to get on an airplane or even in some cases to go inside the airport. You might be surprised to hear that about 25 million Americans suffer from such a powerful form of aerophobia—uh, that's a-e-r-o-, aero, aerophobia—the scientific name for the fear of flying.

So if knowing the facts doesn't help these people, what <u>can</u> help them? Well, research shows that the fastest and most efficient method of treatment is a kind of behavior therapy called desensitization. De-sen-si-ti-zation is the process of becoming less and less sensitive to a stimulus until it no longer affects you. To see how this technique works, let's take the case of a man we'll call . . . Harry. Harry has a problem because he wants a job that requires a lot of traveling, but he's so terrified of flying that just walking into the airport makes him nervous. On the few occasions that he has actually flown, he was so panic-stricken that he was certain he was going to die of a heart attack.

Harry's treatment was divided into two main parts: counseling in the therapist's office and practice in real-life situations. So let's talk about what happened in the therapist's office. First, in Phase 1, Harry learned how to do something called progressive relaxation. This exercise involves tensing and relaxing various muscle groups, beginning with your toes and working up to your head. Maybe you've used this technique when you felt nervous before an exam or if you were having difficulty falling asleep. The purpose of progressive relaxation is to teach you how to control your body. If you have control over your body, you can relax yourself any time you want. And remember, fear of flying is a kind of anxiety . . . so the first thing you want is to eliminate anxiety, to make yourself relaxed.

In the next part of his treatment, Phase 2, Harry's therapist had him make up a list of frightening situations connected with flying. . . to, uh, to list the situations that scared him and arrange them in order from least to most frightening. You can see Harry's list on your handout. Under "Rating", the numbers indicate the level of anxiety that Harry would probably experience in each situation. A number one indicates little anxiety, and a ten indicates high anxiety or even panic.

So, now we come to Phase 3, and this is where Harry's desensitization actually took place. In this stage, the therapist asked him to imagine each situation on the list. For example, imagine dropping a friend off at the airport. So Harry would relax and imagine this scene until he felt no tension or anxiety. Then he would go on to the next item on the list and keep imagining it until he could stay completely relaxed. If he got anxious, he would go back to the previous situation, where he had felt comfortable. He could go back and forth until he was able to comfortably imagine every item or, uh, situation, on the list.

The final phase of therapy took place outside the office, in the real world. Instead of just imagining the situations on the list, desensitization works faster and better if the patient experiences them in real life. So for Harry, this meant actually going to the airport and doing each activity on his list, first with his therapist and then alone. So on the first day, he took a friend to the airport and then turned around and went home. On the next day, he drove to the airport, walked in,

turned around and went home. Then the next time he actually went through the metal detector, and then he went home. And so on. So in each situation, if he felt himself getting anxious, he would use the relaxation technique he had learned until he felt comfortable in that situation.

Harry's entire course of therapy, including the office visits and the practice at the airport, took about two months. By using desensitization, he was able to confront his fear of flying directly and eliminate it. Eventually he became a successful businessman and flew all over the country for his job. In other words, he was cured of his phobia.

CHAPTER 3: LOOKING FOR LOVE

Part One: In Person

Page 52, B. Listening

Exercise 1

Mark: So how do you think your parents would feel if you married someone who wasn't Korean?

Kathy: Uh, we've actually discussed that a lot. Uh, my last boyfriend was Chinese and we had been pretty serious for a while before we broke up. But, um, my attitude had always been, well, I'm more American than I am Korean, so chances are, I'm probably going to meet someone who's not Korean and. . .

M: Oh, yeah.

K: . . . but for my parents, my mom is kind of . . . because my aunt married a Caucasian American, and every time there's a big family gathering, she always felt like he felt left out, and she felt very bad for him. And she didn't want the same to happen to my husband whenever we were with my family, or for me whenever I was with his family.

M: Yeah.

K: So that's her concern. Uh, and my dad just kind of stays out of it. But now, for myself, I'm beginning to go backwards, back to thinking, "Well, you know, I would want my husband to have a close relationship with my parents, so maybe, uh, it would be beneficial if he was Korean and spoke Korean."

K: Well, what about you, Mark? How would your parents feel if you married someone who wasn't of the same religion?

M: Uh, well, I've always thought that it is best to marry someone with the same beliefs as yourself. I mean, I respect other people's religious beliefs, but as far as a romantic relationship, especially a marriage goes, um, I think that a lot of problems can be avoided if you're believing the same way that your partner believes. And, uh, and so, I don't imagine that I would marry outside of my religion because it's a very important part of who I am.

K: Hmm.

Page 53, Exercise 2

1. Um, my attitude had always been, well, I'm more American than I am Korean, so chances are, I'm probably going to meet someone who's not Korean and. . .

2. But for my parents, my mom is kind of, . . . because my aunt married a Caucasian American, and every time there's a big family gathering, she always felt like he felt left out, and she felt very bad for him. And she didn't want the same to happen to my husband whenever we were with my family, or for me whenever I was with his family.

3. Uh, and my dad just kind of stays out of it.

4. But now, for myself, I'm beginning to go backwards, back to thinking, "Well, you know, I would want my husband to have a close relationship with my parents, so maybe, uh, it would be beneficial if he was Korean and spoke Korean."

5. Uh, well, I've always thought that it is best to marry someone with the same beliefs as yourself. I mean, I respect other people's

religious beliefs, but as far as a romantic relationship, especially a marriage goes, um, I think that a lot of problems can be avoided if you're believing the same way as your partner believes. And, uh, and so, I don't imagine that I would marry outside of my religion because it's a very important part of who I am.

Page 54, Exercise 4

a. How d'ya think yer parents'd feel if you married someone who wasn't Korean?

b. I'm probly gonna meet someone who's not Korean.

c. My dad just kinda stays out of it.

d. It would be beneficial if he was Korean 'n' spoke Korean.

Page 54, Exercise 5. Repeat the recording from Exercise 4.

Page 55, Exercise 6

1. How d'ya feel aboutyer English class?

2. It's probly gonna rain this evening.

3. My goal is to learn how to speak, read 'n' write Spanish.

4. Jane's new boyfriend is kinda quiet.

5. My parents'd feel bad if I married a person with a different religion.

Part Two: On the Phone

Page 58, B. Listening

Exercise 1

Linda: Good afternoon. Bright Futures. This is Linda. How may I help you?

Jay: Hi. I'm trying to find out some information about your service.

L: OK. I'll be happy to help you. What's your name?

J: My name's Jay.

L: I'm sorry?

J: Jay. That's j-a-y.

L: All right, Jay. Now, do you mind if I ask you a couple of questions to get us started?

J: Uh, yeah, OK.

L: Good. Now first of all, how did you hear about us?

J: Uh, through a friend.

L: OK, friend. Is your friend a member?

J: No, no, he's, just well, he's trying to help me out, you know, this is, this is kind of embarrassing.

L: Oh, that's OK, we know you're probably too busy to go out there and meet people. . .

J: Yeah, that's basically it.

L: Hmm. Now Jay, can I ask how old you are?

J: I'm twenty-eight.

L: And what do you do?

J: I work in advertising.

L: Advertising. Got it.

L: Uh, OK, so let me tell you what we, what we're about. We're a private membership club for singles. We're not a matchmaking service. I don't know if you know the difference.

J: Uh, no, actually, I don't know the difference.

L: OK. We don't match people up. We don't say, "Jay and Nancy, you know, they both like to play tennis and they both, you know, want three children, so let's stick them together." What we do is we let you choose. And we feel, because we feel that given the opportunity that, you know, adults are intelligent enough to decide for themselves if they want a date.

J: Well, you don't know me.

L: What we do . . . listen, we make it very, very easy. We've been here for more than ten years. And we have over 8,000 members. What we do is we create a pool of quality people to choose from. . .

J: Well, uh, how does it work exactly?

L: Basically how it works is that we have a big library in our office, and in the library there're profiles, photographs, and videotapes.

J: So you come in. . . Well, I don't mean to interrupt, but do you. . .

L: No, no, please. . .

J: . . . you come into the actual place to do the research?

L: Yes. It's a library.

J: OK.

L: And when you come into the library, you'll—we'll—have the profiles, photographs, and videotapes, like I said. And the profile gives the information about them, kind of the bare bones, like if they've been married before, if they have kids, if they drink or smoke, uh, what they do for a living, what they do for fun, uh, what they're looking for in a person. Those sort of general things about people that are really important.

J: OK, so just basically general characteristics.

L: Yeah. And then we also have a five- to six-minute video tape. So you can get an idea of their personality and get a feel for whether or not there'd be any chemistry.

J: And do you make the video. . . I'm sorry, I don't mean to interrupt.

L: Yes, we record them here.

J: OK, you record the videotapes here. Uh, so we have a profile, we have a video, and basically we have all this. . .

L: Photographs, yeah.

J: Yeah, OK. All of this to find the right person? Can I just jump in here? I want to ask about the fee.

L: Uh, that . . . well, let me get to that, too. Let me answer these other points that I hadn't gotten to before.

J: OK.

L: So, uh, yeah, now we're very different you see from Internet dating sites. One, and probably first and foremost, is the fact that we prescreen everybody who walks through here. For the past ten years, we have met every single one of our members.

J: That's good.

L: We know them personally. On the Internet you have to be very careful because a lot of times people lie about a lot of things. Like even if they're married or not, or. . .

J: Well, it sounds like a nice place, it really does. But how much is the fee?

L: Well, this is the thing. . .

: Well, this is the thing. Yeah. You're trying to hook me! Can you tell me how much. . . ?

L: No, no, no, this is the thing; we do not give out our prices over the phone. Because it's corporate policy.

J: Uh-ha.

L: We need to meet you first, we need to determine in person whether or not you're married, and all of those things are done before we extend the membership. We screen you as well as you screening us.

J: Right, right. No, no, no I think that's fine. Can you give me a ballpark figure?

L: There's no such thing.

J: OK. Well, can I call you back? I mean, honestly, I wasn't calling to make an appointment. I was just kind of getting information and . . . Uh, your name's . . .

L: Linda.

J: OK. Then I would prefer calling you back and, and you know, just feeling a little bit more secure about this decision, and then make an appointment.

L: Right. Good, good. But do keep in mind that the best way to get the most information is to see us in person. Do you know where our office is located?

J: Yeah, yeah, I do. Thank you very much.

L: Thank you, Jay. And you have our number. So give me a call if you, if you want to talk more.

J: I certainly will. Thank you very much.

L: Thank you for calling. Bye.

J: Bye.

Page 58, Exercise 3. Repeat the recording from Exercise 1.

Page 60, Exercise 6

1. **Jay:** Well, uh, how does it work exactly?

   Linda: Basically how it works is that we have a big library in our office, and in the library there're profiles, photographs, and videotapes.

   J: So you come in. . . Well, I don't mean to interrupt, but do you. . .

   L: No, no, please. . .

   J: . . . you come into the actual place to do the research?

   L: Yes, it's a library.

2. **J:** OK, you record the videotapes here. Uh, so we have a profile, we have a video, and basically we have all this . . .

   L: Photographs, yeah.

   J: Yeah, OK. All of this to find the right person? Can I just jump in here? I want to ask about the fee.

Page 60, Exercise 8

Example: We're not a matchmaking service.

1. What we do is we let you choose.

2. Let me answer these other points that I hadn't gotten to before.

3. One, and probably first and foremost, is the fact that we prescreen everybody who walks through here.

4. We screen you as well as you screening us.

5. But do keep in mind that the best way to get the most information is to see us in person.

Part Three: On the Air

Page 65, B. Listening

Exercise 1

Susan Stamberg: "Deeply single" is how one writer put it in *To Do List* magazine, and there are plenty of people who are deeply single. Unmarried by choice, living alone by choice, or living together but just not wanting to get married. In Portland, Oregon, Neil Lubow, age fifty-two, has been in a committed relationship for ten years with, as he puts it, "a woman I love, honor, and indulge." And they live separately.

Neil: I'm not against marriage, but I think that marriage is not the only answer. I think it's just one answer. I like my freedom, I like my independence, I like my privacy and my solitude . . ."

SS: Neil Lubow likes living single. In Washington, D.C., Jennifer Schneider, age thirty-one, says most of her thirty-something friends are desperately seeking a someone, but she wonders about marriage all the time.

Jennifer: I'm not sure whether I want to get married or not, or have kids or not.

SS: Hmm. What are your questions?

Jennifer: I'm not sure of the benefits of getting married.

SS: Jennifer Schneider says, "Most people around me, especially the older generation, assume that what is good for me is to have a family." But Jennifer says, "I'm not ready to give in to that assumption." In La Cañada, California, Terri Wild decided when she was fairly young that she didn't want to have children, so she felt the pressure to marry wasn't there. In her early fifties now, Terri Wild has dated over the years, been engaged, made a full circle of friends, and never felt she had to be in a committed relationship to feel fulfilled.

Terri: As I was pursuing my career, as the pool of eligible men dwindled, you know, I found myself sort of making the decision that I wanted to have a full life, and if that didn't necessarily include a husband or a long-term relationship, that was OK. I could still pursue all the things that I wanted to do, and still have a great life. And I feel as though I've pretty much been able to do that.

SS: Do you think there is an assumption in this society that your life is not complete unless you're in some kind of a relationship?

Terri: Yes. I do. I've had a lot of people say, well, you know, "Don't you get lonely, don't you worry about when you're old and alone and there's no one there to take care of you? Don't you get uncomfortable if you wanna go out to dinner and you know, you go out by yourself?" And I suppose there're many people who do worry about those things, and who do feel that way, and you know certainly they're free to make their own choices, but. . .

SS: But you, but that's not you?

Terri: I mean, it doesn't. . . first of all, I get lonely just like any other person does; I don't, I can't think of anything more lonely than being in a marriage or relationship that's not the right one. I think that would be awful.

Page 65, Exercise 3. Repeat the recording from Exercise 1.

Page 66, Exercise 5

SS: In Washington, D.C., Jennifer Schneider, age thirty-one, says most of her thirty-something friends are desperately seeking a someone, but she wonders about marriage all the time.

Jennifer: I'm not sure whether I want to get married or not, or have kids or not.

SS: Hm. What are your questions?

Jennifer: I'm not sure of the benefits of getting married.

SS: Jennifer Schneider says, "Most people around me, especially the older generation, assume that what is good for me is to have a family." But Jennifer says, "I'm not ready to give in to that assumption."

Part Four: In Class

Page 70, B. Listening and Note-Taking

Exercise 2

1. So according to Dr. Fisher, the three stages of love are lust, romantic love, and attachment. **The first stage**, lust, refers to a very powerful physical or sexual attraction to another person.

2. Now, **the second phase of love**, according to Dr. Fisher, is what she calls romantic love.

3. Recent research has shown that high levels of dopamine are in the brains of people who are in love. **For example**, scientists at the

University of London did a very interesting experiment with a group of volunteers who described themselves as being newly in love.

4. **First** the volunteers were shown pictures of their lovers.

5. When the volunteers saw pictures of their lovers, the part of the brain that makes dopamine, this pleasure hormone, was very active. **In contrast**, when they looked at pictures of their friends, there was no such activity.

6. OK. **Now** we come to the third stage of love, what Dr. Fisher calls the attachment phase.

7. So, **let's review** what we've learned so far about the biology of love.

Page 72, Exercise 4

Lecturer: Good afternoon, everyone. The topic of today's lecture is the biology of love. Now that's a strange title, I know, but before I explain it, I'd like you to close your eyes and think about a time when you were *head over heels in love*. Think about the person you were in love with, or, or maybe still are; and remember how it felt, and how you acted. Remember that wonderful, *intense* feeling, when all you could think of was the person you were in love with. OK? Now open your eyes, and push away those wonderful thoughts of love, and instead, focus on three words: testosterone, dopamine, and oxytocin. Testosterone, dopamine, and oxytocin are all *hormones*, which are chemicals that exist in the human brain and change during different stages of love. In recent years scientists have been looking at love not as a feeling or an emotion but rather as a complex biological process. Dr. Helen Fisher, an anthropologist at Rutgers University in New Jersey, believes that love can be divided into three stages, or phases. And scientists have found, and this is my main point, scientists have found that different hormones are active in the brain at each stage of love. So what I'm going to do is describe these three phases, define them, and briefly explain what is going on in our brains as we experience each stage.

So according to Dr. Fisher, the three stages of love are lust, romantic love, and attachment. The first stage, lust, refers to a a very powerful physical or sexual attraction to another person. Now at this stage, scientists have discovered that our brains produce a very high level of the hormone testosterone. We usually think of testosterone as a male hormone. It's the hormone that does give men more muscle, deeper voices, and more hair than women. But testosterone is also found in females in small amounts. It is this hormone that is responsible for the sex drives of both males and females.

Now, the second phase of love, according to Dr. Fisher, is what she calls romantic love. And this is when we become emotionally involved with another person. This is when you feel passionate, romantic, *madly in love*. You can't eat, you can't sleep, and all you can think about is the person you're in love with. At this stage, a different chemical process is happening in the brain, and the important chemical is called dopamine. That's d-o-p-a-m-i-n-e. Dopamine is a hormone which produces a feeling of great pleasure or happiness. And recent research has shown that high levels of dopamine are in the brains of people who are in love. For example, scientists at the University of London did a very interesting experiment with a group of volunteers who described themselves as being newly in love. First the volunteers were shown pictures of their lovers. Then they looked at pictures of people who were just friends, or good friends. And at the same time the scientists used a machine called an MRI scanner to record the activity of different parts of the brain when . . . as the volunteers looked at both sets of pictures. What the scientists found was dramatic. When the volunteers saw pictures of their lovers, the part of the brain that makes dopamine, this pleasure hormone, was very active. In contrast, when they looked at pictures of their friends, there was no such activity. From this, the scientists were able to conclude that dopamine is an essential hormone during the romantic phase of a love relationship.

OK. Now we come to the third stage of love, what Dr. Fisher calls the attachment phase. This is the stage where people normally move in together, they might get married, have children, settle down. And the relationship is characterized by feelings of peace, and security, and stability.

What goes on in the brain at this point? One important hormone that is *associated with* attachment is oxytocin. That's o-x-y-t-o-c-i-n. In research done with animals, scientists have found that animals receiving this hormone tended to attach themselves quickly to partners of the opposite sex. On the other hand, if the hormone was blocked, the animals showed no interest at all in their partners. Now, in humans, oxytocin is found in the blood of both men and women who are involved in stable relationships during times of intimacy. So some scientists think oxytocin may play an important role in the human ability to form close and long-lasting relationships.

So, let's review what we've learned so far about the biology of love. Throughout history people thought of love as an emotion of the heart. But now scientists have shown them that the real organ of love isn't the heart, it's the brain. Testosterone, dopamine, and oxytocin aren't very romantic words, but without them there would be no sex, no love, no romance. Research shows that love is more than just a wonderful feeling. We can also think of it as a biological process just like eating, drinking, or sleeping.

CHAPTER 4: MUSIC TO MY EARS

Part One: In Person

Page 78, B. Listening

Exercise 1

Sarah: My name is Sarah, and I'd have to say my favorite kind of music is jazz. Um, and the reason I like jazz is because there are so many things to it. Um, it can be loud, it can be soft, it can be fast, it can be really slow. Um, there's lots of different kinds of rhythms, and I really like to tap my foot to the beat, um, and I like to hear the rhythms, um, within the music. Uh, there are lots of different instruments like drums and bass, and piano, and guitar, um, and there are shiny instruments like saxophones and trumpets, um, I think it's really fun to watch jazz musicians play music live. Uh, so jazz is my favorite music and that's why.

Kathleen: OK, my first name is Kathleen. My favorite kind of music is, I think is actually bossa nova. And what I like about bossa nova music, bossa nova music is from Brazil, and my favorite artist is Antonio Carlos Jobim. And I find his music the most soothing and inspiring. When I work in my office, and I'm writing and thinking about the things I'm trying to produce, I put on his music. Because it's subtle and soft, it's rhythmic, and it's very soothing, it's soothing to my mind.

Bonnie: My name is Bonnie, and I want to tell you what my favorite kind of music is. My favorite kind of music is classical music. I love classical music. I love orchestras and I love choruses. I love singing classical music myself, I love listening to it myself. Um, I love listening to all the different kinds of instruments in the orchestra— the strings, and the brass, and the woodwinds, and the percussion. Um, I especially love the sound of the strings because to me the strings are the closest to the human voice, which is the most wonderful instrument of all.

Dennis: Hello, my name is Dennis, and, well, I like all kinds of music, but I think my favorite types of music fall into the folk category. And I like it because the, um, I like the down-to-earth quality of the music. You know, it's very honest, and you know I really don't like overproduced music. You know, I like acoustic instruments, piano, guitar, mandolin, all those kinds of stuff, you know. Um, you know I think it's a very American kind of music. That why I, uh, like it, I guess.

Andrea: My name's Andrea and I like rock music. I like most genres. Rock has many different genres and I like most genres of rock except for the loud, screaming rock where, um, you know you just can't understand the words, or, um, you just can't even make out so much as a melody. I like rock where you can hear the words because part of rock music to me is, um, the lyrics and the connection you feel not only to the music but to the lyrics as well.

Spencer: My name is Spencer. Ah, I really, at the moment really like ska. And ska is music that originated in Jamaica, it's kind of Jamaican rock 'n' roll and ska has kind of a reggae beat to it, with a real, um, a real upbeat character to it. Um, I think what I like about ska is the beat. Anything where I can picture the drummer is smiling while playing the drums is something that I really like, and just get your toes tapping to it. And, uh, it's just a lot of fun. And it's just a good-time music. It's the music I like to listen to when I am at the gym or if I'm taking a walk, or especially when I'm cooking.

Page 78, Exercise 2. Repeat the recording from Exercise 1.

Page 79, Exercise 5

1. My name is Sarah, and I'd have to say my favorite kind of music is jazz. Um, and the reason I like jazz is because there are so many things to it. Um, it can be loud, it can be soft, it can be fast, it can be really slow.

2. When I work in my office, and I'm writing and thinking about the things I'm trying to produce, I put on his music. Because it's subtle and soft, it's rhythmic, and it's very soothing, it's soothing to my mind.

3. And I like it because the, um, I like the down-to-earth quality of the music. You know, it's very honest, and you know I really don't like overproduced music.

4. I like most genres. Rock has many different genres and I like most genres of rock except for the loud, screaming rock where, um, you know you just can't understand the words, or, um, you just can't even make out so much as a melody.

Part Two: On the Phone

Page 82, B. Listening

Exercise 1

Message: Thank you for calling the university ticket office. To assure you quality customer service this phone call may be monitored. Please write down the name of the customer service representative who assists you; all messages will play twice.

To order tickets to an event here on campus press 1 now.

For more information about upcoming performing arts programs, athletics, or any other campus event, press 2.

For parking and directions, press 3.

For our office hours, press 5.

If you have a rotary phone, please stay on the line and an Agent will be with you shortly.

Agent:	How can I help you?
Customer:	Hi, um, I wanted some information about the Global Guitars concert on November 21st.
A:	OK, let me get that information for you.
C:	OK.
A:	OK, how can I help you with that?
C:	OK, I just had some general information questions I want to ask before I decide if I want to go to the concert or not. Well, are there still tickets available?
A:	Um, yes there are.
C:	Do you anticipate that this concert's going to be sold out, or do I need to get the tickets right away?
A:	Right now, at this point, there are plenty of seats still available.
C:	OK. And, and, and do you also sell tickets at the door?
A:	Um yes we do.
C:	OK. Can you tell me what the ticket prices are?
A:	Sure. The ticket prices for this event . . . um, there's a top price of 40 dollars, a second price of 30, and a third price of 20.
C:	OK, and for 40 dollars, where do we get to sit?
A:	The 40-dollar price range is, the majority of the bottom level, which is the orchestra level.
C:	Aha. So for 40 dollars you'd have a really good seat.
A:	Yes.
C:	Is there a map of the hall somewhere?
A:	We do have a map online, if you have online access.
C:	Aha.
A:	You could go to www.tickets.ucla.edu.
C:	Oh, OK.
C:	What about parking there?
A:	Yeah, parking is 7 dollars.

C:	OK. Last question: Um, do you, if I buy the tickets, do you have a refund policy there?
A:	Uh we do have a policy of no exchanges, refunds, or cancellations. . .
C:	OK.
A:	After you purchase the tickets.
C:	OK, well, I'm going to give this some thought, and thank you very much for your help.
A:	Oh you're very welcome. Thank you for calling. You have a nice day.
C:	Thanks, you too.
A:	Bye, Bye.
C:	Bye.

Page 82, Exercise 2. Repeat the recording from Exercise 1.

Page 84, Exercise 4

Example: ticket office

1. website
2. office hours
3. ticket prices
4. orchestra level
5. refund policy

Part Three: On the Air

Page 88, B. Listening

Exercise 1

John McChesney, reporting: After years of pursuing file-sharing companies like Napster in court, the Recording Industry Association of America says now it's coming after individuals who make music files available online, perhaps people like a young man named Christian at San Francisco State University, who is striding across campus to a rhythm only he can hear in his headset. He pulls a small MP3 player out of his pocket and turns it off so he can talk. He says he's a heavy Internet music user with 2,200 music tracks on his personal computer. He uses the popular file-sharing software called

Kazaa. So is he worried that the recording industry might come after him?

Christian: No, not at all. I mean, that's a stupid move. I mean, there's no way they can. There's too many people.

JM: There are millions of people sharing music on the Internet, but the recording industry says it will only be suing people who offer "significant numbers," their words, of songs for others to download. Graduate student Judy says she has a staggering 5,000 songs on her hard drive. But she shrugs off the industry's threat to sue people like her.

Judy: I can't imagine that would ever happen. Because I'm just one, you know, IP address and there's millions and millions of others in the United States. They can't crack down on every person. Everyone I know downloads music.

JM: Does she agree with the recording industry that she's stealing music?

Judy: Am I stealing the music? Yeah, technically, I am stealing the music.

JM: And that doesn't trouble you?

Judy: Not really, no. I think they're making enough money from other sources.

JM: Some companies, like Apple, with its iTunes, are now selling downloadable music on the Internet. Apple charges 99 cents for a single track. But Judy says she isn't buying.

Judy: If I was buying them from Apple, you know, that would be 4,000 dollars or 5,000 dollars. That's just too much money to spend on it.

JM: Chris Robeson is a software engineering graduate student but he says he doesn't download music on the Internet.

Chris Robeson: I got some good buddies who are musicians. I'm a musician myself. And I don't want to detract from musicians' abilities to make money, because it's an art, and they deserve to get paid.

Page 88, Exercise 2. Repeat the recording from Exercise 1.

Page 89, Exercise 4

1. come áfter
2. pull óut of
3. turn óff
4. come óut
5. shrug óff
6. crack dówn on

Part Four: In Class

Page 94, B. Listening and Note-Taking

Exercise 2

a. There are dozens of different types of jazz. For instance, there's Latin jazz, Dixieland jazz, free jazz, and ragtime.

b. Rap lyrics can be divided into two broad categories, gangsta rap and soft-core.

c. These days there are more than 20 different subcategories of rap music. For example, there is comedy rap, pop-rap, electro-rap, and many more, and each one has its own distinctive sound.

d. Latin dancing, which has become increasingly popular around the world, can be broken down into several different genres. The most well-known are the salsa, the samba and the tango.

Page 95, Exercise 4

1. Why is it that when we hear a rap song, whether it's in English or Farsi or Korean or French, we immediately know that it's rap? In other words, what are the elements or characteristics that make this style of music so distinctive, uh, so easy to recognize?

2. Well, rap can be defined as a genre of music consisting of rhyming lyrics that are spoken or chanted over a musical background. That is to say, the two essential components of rap are (1) rhyming lyrics and (2) musical accompaniment.

3. Now, the background melody, I mean the tune, is the part that you can sing. And it can be created using any instrument or combination of instruments. Typically, though, in a rap song the melody is not the most prominent or memorable element.

4. The most prominent element is the backbeat, or the rhythm.

Page 96, Exercise 5

Lecturer: OK, um, we've been surveying different styles of modern music and today's topic is rap. Why is it that when we hear a rap song, whether it's in English or Farsi or Korean or French, we immediately know that it's rap? In other words, what are the elements or characteristics that make this style of music so distinctive, uh, so easy to recognize? That's the question I want to answer today.

First of all, what is rap? Well, rap can be defined as a genre of music consisting of rhyming lyrics that are spoken or chanted over a musical background. That is to say, the two essential components of rap are (1) rhyming lyrics and (2) musical accompaniment. Now, I'll be addressing both of these topics but I want to start by looking at the musical aspect.

OK. As you may already know, rap music was started in the 1970s by poor, young, African Americans in New York City. They would go around to parties and dances and rap lyrics over music coming from vinyl records played on an old-fashioned turntable. Now a unique element introduced around 1978 or so was a technique called scratching. And a scratch sound is produced by moving a record back and forth with your hand while it's playing on a turntable. It sounds kind of like *whack-a whack-a whack-a*. And so this unusual sound is something that almost everybody associates with rap music.

Now as time passed, rap music became more sophisticated, and several elements were introduced that we hear until this day. Now, those elements are the background melody, the backbeat, and sampling.

Now the background melody, I mean the tune, is the part that you can sing. And it can be created using any instrument or combination of instruments. Typically, though, in a rap song the melody is not the most prominent or memorable element.

The most prominent element is the backbeat, or the rhythm. Now the backbeat is the repetitive BOOM BOOM BOOM; it's that drum sound that you hear when you're, uh, when you're stopped at a car next to you at a red light. It's one of the most identifiable characteristics of rap music and it is also the thing that makes a lot of people, such as parents, hate it.

All right, so, we have the melody and the backbeat. And then we have a wide range of additional sounds that are mixed in using an electronic device called a sampler, and that's why the technique is called sampling. So, in music sampling refers to taking a portion or a piece of one recording and reusing it in a new recording. So, to give just one interesting example, if you listen to a song called "C U when you get there" by a rap artist named Coolio, you'll hear that the introduction to the song is taken from a 17th century classical composition, the Pachelbel Canon. I'm sure you've heard it, it goes *da da, da . . .* and I will spare you singing the rest of it, OK? But I'm sure that sounds familiar.

All right. That takes care of the musical aspect of rap, so let's now talk a little bit about the lyrics. Now, in general rap lyrics can be divided into two broad categories, gangsta rap and soft-core.

So first, gangsta rap emerged in the early 1980s as a form of protest by young black men wanting to express their frustration at the difficult conditions in America's inner cities. So groups like Public Enemy rapped about their realities and their lives which included drugs, gangs, guns, and violence. Now these rappers used shocking language and spoke about women in very negative terms, so for these reasons gangsta rap was heavily criticized.

Now contrast, by the mid-1990s, as rap music became more and more popular, a second type of lyrics could be heard, and these might be called soft-core. So soft-core rap is much less violent although many songs still emphasize some of the things you'd hear in gangsta rap such as money, cars, jewelry, and other status symbols.

However these days, quite a few rap artists are using their art to promote positive, and encouraging messages. An example is the song "I Can," by Nas, which has the lyric:

I know I can

Be what I wanna be

If I work hard at it

I'll be where I wanna be

Since the mid-1990s rap has entered the mainstream. It is everywhere. Rappers like Ice Cube and Queen Latifah are acting in movies. TV ads for giant companies like McDonald's and Macintosh computers use rap music to sell their products. But perhaps most interesting is the fact that rap has become a worldwide phenomenon. France, for example, has officially declared rap an art form, and it's now the second-largest market for rap music in the world. These days rap's fans come from all social classes, races, and countries. Which is why I would argue, in conclusion, that no other style of music except for possibly rock has brought people together as powerfully as rap has been able to do.

CHAPTER 5: GETTING THE JOB DONE

Part One: In Person

Page 102, B. Listening

Exercise 1

Mike: Hey, Bonnie. Um, I got this extra yogurt here. You want to have it for lunch?

Bonnie: Oh. OK, OK, Mike, thanks a lot, I'm kind of hungry. But there was a time where I really . . . I hated yogurt. I mean. . .

M: Yogurt? What's wrong with yogurt?

B: Well, uh, probably nothing, except you know when I was in college, um, during the summer, I had a summer job and I was promoting yogurt for a major corporation. So, this company would send us to, like, all these marathons around California, and after the runners were through running their 26 miles, we would hand them a yogurt, and they would just eat it really quickly and they would just throw it back, and drink it down, eat it whatever and then, oh. . .

M: Are you serious?

B: Oh, they would get sick! Because they had just run 26 miles! And after that, I tell you. . . And then, the packaging was new. So one time I was in Beverly Hills promoting this yogurt, handing people this yogurt, and the bottoms would fall out on the packaging 'cause it had not been perfected. And all over the, you know these beautiful couture outfits . . . this yogurt went straight down.

M: Was it colorful?

B: It was beautiful, especially the blueberry. Oh, that had to be the worst. What about you, what's your, what was your worst job?

M: The worst job I ever had? I was a night janitor at a, um, at an old people's home once a long time ago.

B: Oh my gosh!

M: And it wasn't that bad of a job but it was so strange because when. . . I would go to work at like 5 o'clock in the evening, and so everybody else is coming home to have dinner, and I'm on my way to work, and I'd, I'd check in and clock in and I'd, you know, punch the clock, and there I'd be. And the place would clear out, and I'm in this big, empty facility and I'd have to go around with my little brush 'n scrub out all the toilets.

B: Oh no!

M: Yeah.

B: Was it depressing?

M: You know, at first it was really depressing. . . I would finish at like 4 o'clock in the morning.

B: Um.

M: And you know I'd be going home tired and the sun is coming up and everybody is just kind of getting up, and I felt so weird, I was so set apart from the whole rest of the world.

B: Like a vampire . . .

M: Yeah, exactly, and I'd go home and go to sleep, and then I'd get up, you know, the next night and go off to clean the toilets again.

B: Again.

M: I lasted I think about two months on that one. I was actually making pretty good money though. So maybe it was worthwhile. And it gave me a chance to be philosophical in the middle of the night.

Page 104, Exercise 4

Bonnie: There was a time where I really hated yogurt.

Mike: Yogurt? What's wrong with yogurt?

B: Probably nothing, except you know when I was in college, um, during the summer, I had a summer job, and I was promoting yogurt for a major corporation . . . And then, the packaging was new. So one time I was in Beverly Hills promoting this yogurt, handing people this yogurt, and the bottoms would fall out on the packaging 'cause it had not been perfected. And all over the, you know these beautiful couture outfits . . . this yogurt went straight down.

Mike: Was it colorful?

Bonnie: It was beautiful, especially the blueberry. Oh, that had to be the worst.

Page 105, Exercise 6. Repeat the recording from Exercise 4.

Page 105, Exercise 8

1. **Bonnie:** . . . after the runners were through running their twenty-six miles, we would hand them a yogurt, and they would just eat it really quickly . . . and they would just throw it back, and drink it down, eat it whatever and then, oh . . .

   Mike: Are you serious?

   Bonnie: They would get sick!

2. **Mike:** The worst job I ever had? I was the night janitor at a, um, at an old people's home once a long time ago.

   Bonnie: Oh my gosh!

3. **Mike:** And the place would clear out, and I'm in this empty facility and I'd have to go around with my little brush 'n scrub out all the toilets.

   Bonnie: Oh no!

   Mike: Yeah.

Part Two: On the Phone

Page 109, B. Listening

Exercise 1

Receptionist: Hello, IBS International.

Scott: Hi. May I speak to Joyce Baker, please?

R: I'm sorry. She's away from her desk. Would you like to leave a message or call her voice mail?

S: Oh, well, I'm just calling to follow up on my job application. I sent, I faxed in my resume last week and I just . . .

R: For which position? We have several. . .

S: Oh, the administrative assistant.

R: Okay. Well, you'll need to talk to Ms. Baker about that. Does she have your number?

S: Yes, it's on the resume. But could you give it to her anyway?

R: Sure.

S: All right. I'm Scott Williams and I'm at 310-555-1212.

R: Okay, I'll give her the message. Oh, wait, she just stepped in. I'll transfer you. Can you hold?

S: Oh yes, thanks very much.

Ms. Baker: Hello, this is Joyce. Can I help you?

S: Oh, Ms. Baker? Uh, hi, this is Scott Williams. I faxed in my application for the administrative assistant position last week. I was just wondering if you've had a chance to . . . look it over.

Ms. B.: Oh, yeah, yeah, uh, hi, Scott. I've read it, yeah, um. . . . Actually I was gonna call you 'cause I do have a couple of questions. Let's see. . . Let me locate it here, um, among my piles. . . OK, here it is. Yeah, your qualifications seem pretty strong. . . good computer skills. . . OK, so I was wondering: What can you tell me, a little bit please about your international experience.

S: Sure, um . . . I've done some traveling abroad, and actually I lived in Mexico for six months where I was at. . .

Ms. B.: Yes, but Scott excuse me, but have you worked with international clients, I mean a diverse population like we have here?

S: Oh, uh, well, when I worked in the Study Abroad department at the university. . . uh, about a year ago. . . I worked with lots of overseas representatives. . . you know. . . the people that our students dealt with when they studied in Germany and France and Spain. . .

Ms. B.: OK, I see. Good. So, what exactly were your responsibilities in that job?

S: Uh, well, a variety of things. Uh, it involved a lot of problem solving, you know, uh, with the students being overseas for the first time, and making sure things went smoothly. . . So, a lot of phone work was involved, uh, correspondence by e-mail, fax and stuff like that. And uh, also, I was responsible for billing. . . so I worked with the parents of the students as well.

Ms. B.: OK, well, it sounds like you're pretty good at multitasking. . .

S: Oh, yeah, definitely multitasking. . . it was a very busy office, with constant interruptions and everything, but , uh, I kind of like that. . . it kept things interesting. . .

Ms. B.: OK, well I, I get the picture. Uh, just one other thing here. I see that you live in Studio City. . . that's kind of . . . well, about how long a commute is that?

S: Oh. Uh, y-yeah, well, um, it's a pretty long commute, I guess, maybe thirty or forty minutes. But, that shouldn't be a problem, really.

Ms. B.: Well, I'm just a little concerned about that. . . Well, you know what? Why don't we just schedule an interview so we can talk a little more in detail about. . .

S: Ah, that would be great. Uh, I'm available any time actually.

Ms. B.: Oh good, well how about, uh, let me check here . . . How about Wednesday at two?

S: OK, Wednesday at two. Sure, that sounds good. And. . . you're in suite 300, right?

Ms. B.: Yeah, that's right. OK, good. Um, well I'll look forward to meeting with you, Scott.

S: Me too, thanks very much. . . See you on Wednesday.

Ms. B.: See you then. Bye bye.

S: Bye.

Page 110, Exercise 2. Repeat the recording from Exercise 1.

Page 111, Exercise 4

1.   **Scott:** Oh, well, I'm just calling to follow up on my job application. I sent, I faxed in my resume last week. . . .

2.   **Ms. B.:** Hello, this is Joyce. Can I help you?

       S: Oh, Ms. Baker? Uh, hi, this is Scott Williams. I faxed in my application for the administrative assistant position last week. I was just wondering if you've had a chance to . . .

3.   **S:** . . . also, I was responsible for billing . . . so I worked with the parents of the students as well.

4.   **Ms. B.:** OK, well, it sounds like you're pretty good at multitasking. . .

       S: Oh, yeah, definitely multitasking. . .

5.   **Ms. B.:** OK, well I, I get the picture. Uh, just one other thing here. I see that you live in Studio City. . . that's kind of . . . well, about how long a commute is that?

       S: Oh. Uh, y-yeah, well, um, it's a pretty long commute, I guess, maybe thirty or forty minutes. . . but, that shouldn't be a problem, really. . .

Part Three: On the Air

Page 115, B. Listening

Exercise 1

Interviewer: Tell me with some very practical situations here. For instance, let me get your impression of. . . you make a call, and a person picks up using the speakerphone. Is this proper etiquette? Are you allowed to use the speakerphone?

Peggy Post: Well, you're certainly allowed to. But the way to use it is to ask the other person, "Do you mind if I use a speaker phone?" That's the polite, courteous, considerate thing to do. Another thing is, if there are other people in the room, the main person who's speaking should identify the other people in the room. Say, "I just want you to know that Mary Williams is here with me, and David Jones." And they should also say hello.

Interviewer: All right, another pet peeve: forwarding e-mail. Let's say, Peggy, I send you some e-mail. And then, without asking, you think it's quite interesting, you send it on to Peter. I didn't know Peter was going to get it. Is that all right? Should you forward without asking the original originator of the e-mail message?

Peggy: That's a reality in our e-mail world out there. So we do like to point out that if it's something that you want to keep confidential or private or you really were hoping only one person is going to see, it's better not to e-mail that because it is so easy for people to pass it along.

Interviewer: So you're counseling, "Know that it's probably going to get forwarded, and don't put anything in an e-mail that would really be a problem if it were forwarded."

Peggy: Yes, we think that's good advice.

Interviewer: Now, you have a section in the book about leaving your job. And you write that if you've been fired or asked to resign, not only should you not leave mad, but you shouldn't leave the impression that you're mad. I mean, hey, someone fires me, you're going to be mad.

Peggy: Right.

Interviewer: And, uh, what's the point of trying to repress your feelings in that situation?

Peggy: Well, you may certainly be mad and not repress those feelings in private. But the point is, again, be professional, and be as calm and poised as you possibly can with the person who is firing you, with the people around you. It is all about not wanting to burn bridges.

Interviewer: Let's turn that around. What about if you were the boss who's just received an unexpected resignation letter?

Peter: You want to maintain your poise, you want to wish the person well, you want to thank them for all that they've done for your company, and you're likely to gain more long-term benefit out of doing that than yelling at the person and throwing them out of your office, which I don't think would accomplish any good for anybody.

Page 116, Exercise 2. Repeat the recording from Exercise 1.

Part Four: In Class

Page 121, B. Listening and Note-Taking

Exercise 2

Lecturer: Good morning, everybody. Uh, the question I want to address today is why Americans work as hard as they do. Now, we've already seen that Americans work almost as many hours per year as the Japanese and Koreans. And compared to Europeans, well, Americans work three to four hundred hours a year more than people in Western Europe. They take fewer vacations and they retire at a later age. Why is this? How do you explain that? That's what I want to talk about for the next few minutes.

Page 123, Exercise 4

1. And compared to Europeans, well, Americans work three to four hundred hours a year more than people in Western Europe. They take fewer vacations and they retire at a later age. Why is this? How do you explain that?

2. But the main reason why Americans work as hard... why Americans work hard is that the U.S. economic structure rewards them for it, and Americans see this as a good thing.

3. In other words, people work harder because they know that in most cases the hard work will lead to higher pay.

4. In Europe, on the other hand, the wage gap, I mean the difference in salary between the highest and the lowest salaries in the company, is generally much smaller than in the U.S., so people in Europe have less of an incentive to work hard.

5. Technology actually causes people to work more than they did twenty or thirty years ago.

Page 124, Exercise 5

Lecturer: Good morning, everybody. Uh, the question I want to address today is why Americans work as hard as they do. Now, we've already seen that Americans work almost as many hours per year as the Japanese and Koreans. And compared to Europeans, well, Americans work three to four hundred hours a year more than people in Western Europe. They take fewer vacations and they retire at a later age. Why is this? How do you explain that? That's what I want to talk about for the next few minutes.

Now there are many reasons why Americans work as hard as they do. One reason has to do with American history. The Europeans who first settled this country were religious Christians who believed in the value of hard work, and that value has stayed with us to this day.

But the main reason why Americans work as hard... why Americans work hard is that the U.S. economic structure rewards them for it, and Americans see this as a good thing. Let me explain to you what I mean. In the U.S. there is a very wide range of salaries, wages, within companies, much wider than in other... in most other countries. For example the president of a big U.S. company can earn anywhere from 50 to 100 times more than an average worker. Now, my point isn't to say that this is unfair, though I think it is and many people think it is. The advantage of a system like this is that it creates incentives for employees to work harder. In other words, people work harder because they know that in most cases the hard work will lead to higher pay. In Europe, on the other hand, the wage gap, I mean the difference in salary between the highest and the lowest salaries in the company, is generally much smaller than in the U.S., so people in Europe have less of an incentive to work hard.

So obviously most people work hard in order to make as much money as possible. And a third reason, which is related to the previous one, the one I just mentioned, is that a lot of people work hard to keep a job that gives them benefits. By benefits I mean things like medical insurance, unemployment insurance, and a retirement plan. Now in most European countries, these things are paid for by the government, so people are protected even if they lose their jobs. But in contrast, in the U.S., benefits are normally paid by a person's employer. What that means is that in the United States, if you lose your job, you also lose your benefits. So people are willing to work as hard as necessary in order to hold on to jobs that offer benefits.

Another reason why Americans work hard is technology. You might be surprised to hear that because technology's supposed to make it possible for people to work less, to give them more free time, right? But here's the paradox: Technology actually causes people to work more than they did twenty or thirty years ago. Now how is that so? That's because with e-mail and voicemail

and videoconferencing and telecommuting and all the other high-tech methods of communication we have these days, it's so easy to stay in touch with the office that there's almost an expectation that people will check in even if they're on vacation. And because good jobs are hard to find these days, people might feel that they have to do it, that they feel pressured to stay in touch even if they don't want to. So you see how technology sometimes forces people to work harder and longer, whether they want to or not.

Now it might seem that Americans work hard for a lot of negative reasons, but there's one more reason I want to mention that I think is positive. And that is that many people work hard for the simple reason that they enjoy it! For many Americans, their work gives them an identity, meaning they say "I'm a teacher," "I'm a bus driver," "I'm a something." Work gives these people a sense of purpose or accomplishment, or maybe they enjoy the feeling of being part of a team. By the way, a common question that gets asked in job interviews in this country is "Are you a team player?" So this is something that Americans clearly value. Anyway, my point is that millions of Americans work hard because work gives them personal rewards that go beyond just money.

So to sum up, you can see that there are a variety of reasons why Americans work hard—historical, economic, and personal. For many people work is a rewarding experience that gives them great satisfaction. Other people work out of necessity, because they have to. Where work becomes a problem is when it starts affecting people's health and family life, and that's what we're gonna talk about next.

CHAPTER SIX: TO YOUR HEALTH!

Part One: In Person

Page 130, B. Listening

Exercise 1

Bene: Lisa, is that you? [Lisa: Hey, how are you doing?] I haven't seen you in the longest time.

Lisa: I know. What you are doing here? Usually you're not here in the mornings.

B: Yeah, well um, you know how I've got my regular evening class, right.

L: Right.

B: But one of the teachers called in sick, and I didn't have anything to do this morning, so they asked me to come in.

L: Oh, so, well it's really good to see you.

B: You seem a little bit. . . sad, or something. Is everything all right?

L: Oh yeah, it's OK, I'm just pretty bummed out. I had to get rid of my cat.

B: Oh no, what happened? That sounds awful.

L: Well, it is pretty awful. I actually found out that I was allergic.

B: Really? How allergic?

L: Um, pretty allergic, so about three months ago I started feeling pretty out of it, and I didn't really think about, you know that I had the cat, I didn't really make that association, so. . .

B: And so you just recently got this cat.

L: Yeah.

B: OK.

L: I had just gotten the cat probably a couple of weeks before.

B: Oh, OK. And so you went to a doctor, or . . . how did you find out whether, what were your symptoms?

L: Um, yeah, so I started, I was just feeling really lethargic, and I didn't have any energy, and you know I was sneezing a lot, and my eyes were really itchy and irritated, and I had headaches . . .

B: That sounds pretty serious.

L: Yeah, well, at first I thought I was just coming down with a cold, um . . .

B: Right.

L: But the symptoms just went from bad to worse, and so I finally went to the doctor,

B: So did they run any tests on you, what, what what did they do?

L: Well I had told him that I had, you know, when I thought about it after a while when I couldn't figure out you know what possibly could be wrong, after I knew it wasn't just a cold, and I was like "Oh, I just got this cat not long before." And so the doctor said, "You know, well, you know we should run some tests to see if you're allergic."

B: Hmm hmm.

L: Um, and yeah, it was confirmed so I had this allergy to cats, so I was . . .

B: You're kidding . . .

L: No, and I was shocked because I had never. . . you know I had been around cats, I had never had my own but I had been . . .

B: Right.

L: . . . around cats . . .

B: That's really surprising.

L: . . . in others' homes. Yeah, I was really surprised. Um, and so it turns out that it's not just cats, but it's dust and mold and pollen and anything airborne and it was. . . I know . . .

B: That's too much. How do you get away from all of that then?

L: I don't know so I was like really worried 'cause I thought, you know, you hear about these bad cases of asthma, and it sort of starts from these like you know allergic reactions, so I was really kind of . . .

B: Yeah, I know, so it sounds like it was a good thing that you went in to see the doctor. Did he prescribe any sort of treatment or medication?

L: Yeah, at first I tried some pills that they had prescribed, but they made me really sleepy.

B: Were they able to give you an alternative?

L: Yeah, so now I'm taking this nasal spray twice a day, so it's a little bit better.

B: So it's helping you, then?

L: It's helping, yeah, I'm just not thrilled about taking medicine forever.

B: Yeah, who is!

L: Right, yeah, exactly, so there's no cure for allergies so it seems that this is right now the best choice I have, so—

B: It's too bad though that you had to lose your cat.

L: Yeah, I was really, I was really bummed out about it.

Page 130, Exercise 2. Repeat the recording from Exercise 1.

Page 131, Exercise 6

1. One of the teachers called in sick, and I didn't have anything to do this morning, so they asked me to come in.

2. I'm just pretty bummed out. I had to get rid of my cat.

3. I actually found out that I was allergic.

4. About three months ago I started feeling pretty out of it.

5. I had just gotten the cat probably a couple of weeks before.

Page 132, Exercise 7

1. And so you went to a doctor, or. . . how did you find out whether, what were your symptoms?

2. Um, yeah, so I started, I was just feeling really lethargic, and I didn't have any energy, and you know I was sneezing a lot, and my eyes were really itchy and irritated, and I had headaches . . .

3. Well, at first I just thought I was just coming down with a cold . . .

4. Well I had told him that I had, you know, when I thought about it after a while when I couldn't figure out you know what possibly could be wrong, after I knew it wasn't just a cold, and I was like "Oh, I just got this cat not long before."

5. And so the doctor said, "You know, well, you know we should run some tests to see if you're allergic."

Part Two: On the Phone
Page 136, B. Listening

Exercise 1

Pharmacist: Pharmacy, may I help you?

Caller: Uh, hi. Uh, I have a question. I'm having a lot of trouble falling asleep, and I left a message for my physician, and then she called me back, uh, and left a message saying it's OK to take Benesec once in a while.

P: Hmm.

C: Yeah, but I didn't get a chance to talk to her in person, and uh I'm confused 'cause I usually use Benesec for allergies?

P: Uh, well it's true but one of the side effects of Be- of Benesec is drowsiness, so uh lots of over-the-counter medications to help you sleep, they, they all contain uh antihistamines. . . and uh the antihistamines in general, they make you sleepy, so a lot of people use it for sleep even though it's not a sleeping, you know, a medicine or medication, strictly speaking.

C: Yes, but is it safe to do that?

P: Uh yeah absolutely. Now it might dry you out a little bit because it—it is an antihistamine but, other than that it should be fine.

C: Uh, but what about the long-term effects. . . is it like habit-forming?

P: No, no it's not, but what I'm concerned about is that you're. . . you're having difficulty sleeping?

C: Yeah.

P: So yeah, you can use this but, you know, it's it's, if it's every night you may have to find out what the cause of your sleeplessness is, and uh, but if it's just occasionally then I wouldn't worry. . .

C: Oh, OK. Um, yeah, you know, I'm really worried about taking drugs to make me sleep. . . you know, is there some natural remedy or plant or herb or something I can take?

P: Well, yeah there are but they're not anything I can recommend.

C: Yeah?

P: Yeah, you're really safer with the Benesec.

C: Really? How come?

P: Well, uh they could have some side effects that we're not sure about. . .

C: Hmm.

P: . . .so I never recommend, uh, we never recommend herbs.

C: OK. Well thanks for your time.

P: Oh, you're welcome.

Page 137, Exercise 2

Segment 1

P: . . . antihistamines in general, they make you sleepy, so a lot of people use it for sleep even though it's not a sleeping you know, a medicine or medication, strictly speaking.

Caller: Yes, but is it safe to do that?

Segment 2

P: . . . It might dry you out a little bit because it—it is an antihistamine but, other than that it should be fine.

Segment 3

P: . . . what I'm concerned about is that you're . . . having difficulty sleeping? So yeah, you can use this, but, you know, it's it's if it's every night you may have to find out what the cause of your sleeplessness is, and uh, but, if it's just occasionally then I wouldn't worry. . .

Segment 4

P: Well, yeah there are but they're not anything I can recommend.

C: Yeah?

P: You're safer with the Benesec.

Caller: Really? How come?

P: Well, uh they could have some side effects that we're not sure about. . .

C: Hmm.

P: . . .so I never recommend, uh, we never recommend herbs.

Page 138, Exercise 4

1. **Woman:** Betsy has had a fever for a couple of days. I'm worried that she might have an infection, or . . .

   Friend: Oh, there's no need to worry. Little kids get fevers all the time. They usually disappear after a day or two.

2. **Father:** What happened to you! There's a big black bruise on your face!

   Son: Don't get excited, Dad. It's not a bruise. It's paint.

3. **Student:** I'm really scared that I'm going to fail this economics test. I just don't get this stuff.

   Roommate: I wouldn't worry if I were you. Professor Martin's tests aren't that hard.

4. **Woman:** I'm not real comfortable with that funny noise the car is making.

   Man: I'm sure it's nothing serious, but I'll have a mechanic take a look.

Part Three: On the Air

Page 142, B. Listening

Exercise 1

Radio reporter Stephanie Ho: U.S. health officials say there is a new epidemic; it's called obesity. The World Health Organization says the problem is global. Obesity is linked to a number of serious health problems, such as cancer, heart disease, hypertension and diabetes. As diets higher in fat and sugar become more widely available around the globe, fighting fat is not just a U.S. problem.

The 2000 National Health and Nutrition Examination Survey, prepared by the Centers for Disease Control and Prevention, found that nearly two-thirds of Americans over the age of twenty are overweight, and more than thirty percent are obese.

The American Obesity Association says these percentages translate into approximately 127 million American adults who are overweight, 60 million who are obese, and 9 million who are severely obese.

Why are so many Americans overweight? Barbara Rolls, from Pennsylvania State University, says part of the problem is the American diet.

"We have a huge variety of foods that are inexpensive. They're readily available. They're high in fat, high in energy density, and they're in huge portions."

Dietitian Jackie Newgent says too much of a good thing is bad for health.

She says American fastfood giants are making inroads into other countries around the world. "It's unfortunate that, for instance, the Asian diet and the European diet, they may have started as healthier diets, and they are becoming more Americanized, which actually means they are going to get a little bit more saturated fat, and likely more trans-fat. I don't know what the stats are on that, but that is definitely a trend."

The World Health Organization calls obesity an escalating global epidemic that it has dubbed "globesity."

WHO statistics say the number of obese adults worldwide jumped from 200 million to 300 million, between 1995 and 2000. The health organization also points to the rise in childhood obesity, estimating that more than 17.5 million children under the age of five are overweight around the world.

Page 142, Exercise 2. Repeat the recording from Exercise 1.

Page 142, Exercise 3. Repeat the recording from Exercise 1 again.

Page 143, Exercise 6

1. Doctors in Boston report that the traditional Chinese martial art Tai Chi appears to have health benefits for older patients.

2. According to scientists from the Tokyo University Hospital, greater consumption of coffee tends to reduce the risk of adult diabetes.

3. Medical researchers found that antibacterial soaps and cleansers do not prevent disease.

4. Health risks from current genetically modified foods are very low, says a report recently published by the British government.

5. A study done at the University of Wisconsin suggests that drinking green tea may be helpful in treating certain kinds of cancer.

Part Four: In Class

Page 150, B. Listening, and Note-Taking

Exercise 4

Lecturer: Um, as a nutritionist, the most frequently asked question I hear in my practice is, "What is the most effective diet?" And as we all know, one of the big reasons I'm asked this is that obesity has become a major problem in this country recently. In fact, in twenty years of practice, I have, unfortunately, seen an increasing number of overweight people. And most sadly, more and more children these days are overweight. Now, we all know that there is no shortage of advice on how to lose weight. Um, if you open any magazine, if you go on the Internet, or whatever, you are just bombarded with ads for an amazing variety, for all kinds of diets. You have the grapefruit diet, you have the cabbage soup diet, you have the famous Atkins diet, and you have the raw food diet and it just goes on and on. Um, let me tell you first that most of these are just fads. And that there is simply not enough scientific data to back up these diets.

However, two diets that have been around a long time and that seem to work are the low-fat diet and the low-carb diet, or low-carbohydrate diet. So these are the two I want to discuss today. Um, let's think about how they're different, or let me talk about how they're different and how they really work.

First of all, let's look at the low-fat diet. This requires that you cut back on foods that are high in fats and oils. How are you going to do this?

You are going to cut back on meats, especially red meats, cheeses, butter, and fried foods of all kinds. Now that may sound very healthy. And you are probably thinking, "If I cut down on fats, I won't get fat!" Plus it will lower my cholesterol and that will prevent heart disease." That's fine. But in terms of weight loss, is it effective in the long term?

Here are some of the problems with this kind of diet. First, you have to restrict your choice of food. And what happens is, people get bored eating the same thing over and over. Then they get frustrated. And they stop eating what they're supposed to eat on the diet. Then they get hungry and they overeat on certain other foods, like high-calorie foods and foods high in sugar. So they end up gaining back most of the weight that they've lost. And that is the main drawback.

Now, the other diet I mentioned was the low-carb diet. This is very popular in recent years, and in some ways is just the opposite of the low-fat diet. In contrast to the low-fat diet, with the low-carb diet you restrict your intake of carbohydrates, not fats. You know what carbohydrates are, right? This is the substance, or component, of food that gives your body heat and energy. So what foods are high in carbohydrates? Well, sugary foods and starches, things like sweets, breads, pastas, potatoes, rice and corn. You're supposed to stay away from all of these. That's because there are so many carbohydrates in these foods that the body can only use some of them for energy, and the rest it will store as, you guessed it, fat.

Some low-carbohydrate diets, like the famous Atkins diet, are a little extreme. Um, the Atkins diet wants you to eliminate fruits, fruit juices, and even some vegetables. Why? Because these foods are high in carbohydrates. So if you stop eating these foods, you're going to lose weight really fast. And that's a big advantage of this diet. But there're some health concerns. And this is a big "but" with this kind of diet. Nutritional experts worry about the effects of low-carb diets on the body. What kind of effects are we talking about? Some significant ones, like vitamin deficiencies, dehydration, kidney problems, and some others.

So these two diets, the low-carb diet and the low-fat diet, sound very different; however, they are also similar in some important ways. First, both limit your food choices. Second, both of these diets are difficult to stay on for a long period of time. And finally, according to several studies, people either begin cheating on the diet, or they go off the diet completely. And they gain the weight back, sooner or later.

So, to go back to my question at the beginning of the lecture, what do I tell my patients who want to know what the best diet is? Well, my best weight-loss advice is: first, eat sensibly. And second, get off the couch. What I mean by that is, you should reduce the calories that you eat, but you also need to eat a well-balanced diet. That includes proteins, carbohydrates and fats. In other words, eat from every food group, but control the size of your portions. However, I really want to emphasize that you also need to use more calories than you eat. You need to be active and you need to exercise several times a week. Now I know this is not glamorous, or new or particularly exciting, but if you are really interested in improving your health, if you really want long-term weight management, if these are your goals, then this is the best approach for you.

CHAPTER SEVEN: SHOP 'TIL YOU DROP

Part One: In Person

Page 155, B. Listening

Exercise 1

Salesperson: May I help you?

Customer: Yes, I bought this leather jacket here last week, and the zipper broke the first time I wore it.

Salesperson: Hmm.

C: See?

S: I'm sorry about that. Uh, d'ya have the receipt?

C: Yeah, right here.

S: OK. Well, wouldja like ta exchange the jacket fer another one?

C: Well, it was on sale, and I just checked; there aren't any more. This was the last one.

S: Oh no. . . . Didjawanna get something else?

C: No, I don't think so. Uh, I'd like to just get my money back.

S: I'm really sorry but we don't give refunds on sale items. . . we'll exchange it or give you a store credit in this case since the merchandise was defective, but, um, that's store policy, no refunds on sale items.

C: What? Excuse me, but nobody told me that when I bought the jacket, so how was I supposed to know?

S: Well, it's on the sign right next to the cash register. . . .

C: You don't really think anybody reads that, do you? Look, could I talk to the manager?

S: Sure, I'll get her for you.

Page 155, Exercise 2

Manager: Hi, I'm Cheryl. How can I help you?

Customer: I bought this jacket last week and the zipper broke. I'd like to get my money back but I'm told your store doesn't give refunds.

M: It was on sale?

C: Yeah.

M: Then I'm afraid that's right.

C: But I didn't know that when I bought the jacket or I never would've bought it!

M: I'm really sorry but that's the company policy.

C: Look, it's my first time shopping here. Couldn'tcha give me a break just this once?

M: I wish I could, but it is the company policy, so my hands are tied.

C: Well what if I wrote a letter to company headquarters?

M: You're welcome to try, but frankly, I think you'd be wasting your time. They'll just tell you the same thing.

C: This is such a ripoff.

M: Would you like me to help you find something else?

C: I can't afford to get anything else here. Everything costs a fortune! I only got this jacket because it was on sale!

M: I'm really very sorry. All I can do is give you a store credit, and I can give you 10 percent off on your next purchase. Would that help?

C: I don't have a choice, do I?

M: Let's go back to the register and I'll ask one of the clerks to help you.

C: OK. Thanks.

Page 156, Exercise 3

Listen to Exercise 1 and Exercise 2 again.

Page 157, Exercise 5

1. Wouldja like ta exchange the jacket fer another one?

2. Didjawanna get something else?

3. I'd like tuh jus' get my money back.

4. I'll getter for you.

5. I didn't know that when I bought the jacket or I never would've bought it.

6. Couldn'tcha gimme a break just this once?

Part Two: On the Phone

Page 162, B. Listening

Exercise 1

Phone call Number One

Rental Agent: Best Deals Car Rentals. How can I help you?

Customer: Hi. I'm calling to get some information about your rates.

RA: I can help you with that. When, uh, when did you need the car?

C: Well, I have some relatives. . . uh, relatives visiting next month from Italy.

RA: OK.

C: Uh, so I just wanted to know if you have daily rates, or weekly rates or. . .

RA: We have both and monthly.

C: Uh, can you tell me what they are?

RA: Yeah. Do you know what size car?

C: Well, it's four people, so what, uh, what are the different options?

RA: Well, a mid-size car for us is like a Ford Focus or a Toyota Corolla.

C: Uh-huh.

RA: And that's 39 dollars a day.

C: OK.

RA: 190 a week and 650 a month.

C: I see.

RA: Would you like me to reserve one for you?

C: Uh, well, not—not yet, I mean I'm —I'm trying to see which company is best for them.

RA: Well, we're very competitive on our pricing.

C: OK.

RA: Yeah, that's number one. Second, is our service. We provide free pick-up and/or delivery, anywhere, wherever you need it. And the rates I just quoted you do include unlimited mileage.

C: Oh, they do?

RA: Yup.

C: Because I did see cheaper rates um somewhere, but maybe those didn't include unlimited mileage.

RA: Yeah, and they probably have older vehicles. So pretty much the 190 a week for new vehicles is the best I could do. But if they rent over the weekend, we <u>do</u> have weekend specials as well.

C: Um, weekend specials. What are they?

RA: Those run from Friday to Monday, and the mid-size car with the unlimited mileage would be 30 bucks a day.

C: I see. Well, that sounds good.

RA: Yeah, those are kind of our options as far as. . .

C: Well, I'm sorry . . . but do those rates include insurance?

RA: No, they don't.

C: Oh, they don't? How much extra. . .?

RA: It's 11.99 a day.

C: Uh-huh. And is tax included, or is that extra, too?

RA: Tax is not included. Tax is extra: 8.25 percent.

C: And is that OK if they don't have a local driver's license?

RA: Uh, yeah, it's fine. As long as they have a valid driver's license from somewhere.

C: Uh-hmm. And can everyone in the family drive the car? 'Cause they have two children . . .

RA: You can have up to three drivers max. And everyone who drives has to show a driver's license and a credit card.

C: And what about an age limit? I think they have an eighteen-year-old and a twenty-two-year-old.

RA: We rent to twenty-one and up. The eighteen-year-old would not be able to drive.

C: I see. Well, uh, you've been very helpful. Thanks very much.

RA: You're welcome. Just give me a call when you're ready to reserve. My name's Erik.

C: Thanks Erik. I will give you a call.

RA: OK. Bye.

C: Bye.

Page 162, Exercise 1

Phone call Number Two

Rental
Agent 2: Discount Cars. May I help you?

Customer: Hi. Can you tell me about your rates, please?

RA 2: Sure, I'd be glad to. What kind of car are you interested in?

C: Actually, it's not for me. I'm expecting some visitors from Italy, so I'm just shopping around for them.

RA 2: OK. How many people?

C: Four. It's a family of four.

RA 2: I see. So are we looking at a mid-size car, a mini-van, or an SUV?

C: A mid-size would be fine.

RA 2: Mid-size is 249 per week. That includes everything: tax, insurance, and unlimited mileage.

C: Okay. What about per day?

RA 2: We rent for a one-week minimum. Then after one week, the additional days are 45 dollars per day.

C: Is that your lowest rate?

RA 2: Let's see. We've got a promotional package, the Las Vegas Special. It's 119 for three days, with 600 free miles.

C: Oh, that might be good for them. Um, and does that include insurance as well or is that extra?

RA 2: Yes. All the insurance is included.

C: Oh, OK. Um, and about the drivers, what's your policy about drivers under twenty-one?

RA 2: Well, we don't rent to anyone under twenty. Do they have teenagers?

C: Uh, I think their kids are eighteen and twenty-two.

RA 2: Okay, well, twenty is the minimum and there's a surcharge of 5 dollars for under twenty-five.

C: 5 dollars extra per day?

RA 2: Yes, that's right.

C: So anyone in the family can drive the car as long as they are over twenty.

RA 2: Yes.

C: All right. Well, I think that's all I need to know for now. Thanks very much for your help.

RA 2: You're welcome. Thanks for calling Discount Cars.

C: Bye.

Page, 162, Exercise 2. Each group should repeat the recording from Exercise 1.

Page 163, Exercise 5

1. How can I help you?
2. May I help you?
3. When, uh, when did you need the car?
4. Do you know what size car?
5. Uh what are the different options?
6. Would you like me to reserve one for you?
7. Oh, they do?
8. And is tax included, or is that extra, too?
9. And is that OK if they don't have a local driver's license?
10. What kind of car are you interested in?
11. How many people?
12. So are we looking at a mid-size car, a mini-van, or an SUV?
13. What about per day?
14. Is that your lowest rate?
15. What's your policy about drivers under twenty-one?
16. 5 dollars extra per day?

Part Three: On the Air

Page 168, B. Listening

Exercise 1

Interviewer: Barry Schwartz is the author of *The Paradox of Choice—Why More Is Less*. He says the proliferation of consumer goods can give even the best shopper an anxiety attack.

Barry Schwartz: You go to buy a new cell phone and encounter thirty or forty different models with twenty or thirty different faces and twenty five or thirty different plans available—all of them in just one cell phone store. And then you go to buy a digital camera and face the . . . how many megapixels, and optical zoom, digital zoom, what brand, what software, does weight matter? I know what I do in situations like that is I escape and keep whatever I've had; decide that it will serve me one more year.

I: You've identified two types and two different methods of making a decision.

BS: We've distinguished people who are satisfied with "good enough" when they make decisions—we call them "satisfizers"—from people who feel the need to have the best; we call them "maximizers." The problem of having all this choice is particularly acute if you're a maximizer because the only way really to know that you've got the best is if you've examined all of the alternatives. You can't possibly examine all of the alternatives with respect to anything of any consequence. And so the result is, eventually you stop looking, you make a decision, and you're plagued with doubt that if you'd looked a little longer or gone to a different store, you'd have found something better than what you ended up with.

I: What about the "satisfizers"?

BS: What it means to be a "satisfizer" is that you have standards of what's good enough. They're internal standards; you don't need to worry about what other people are doing. And you look for a cell phone or a digital camera that meets those standards. And as soon as you find one, you choose it and stop the search.

I: Well, clearly, this is the way to go. The satisfizers can get on with their lives.

BS: Even satisfizers are really challenged by the amount of choice. But it's possible to cope if your standards are reasonable.

I: But choice is good, we're told, because it forces the makers to come up with a better product and a lower price.

BS: That's absolutely true. And you've hit on a very deep part of the ideology of this country. You know, that ideology has governed this society at least since, since Reagan was president. And it's based on the following assumption: Some choice is good—there's no denying it. But then if some choice is good, then it must be true that more choice is better. That piece of the assumption, I think, we're now showing to be false. Yes, some choice is good, but no, more choice isn't better, or at least isn't always better.

Page 169, Exercise 4

1. go to buy a digital camera
2. thirty or forty different models
3. more choice is better
4. get on with their lives
5. the way to go
6. what I do
7. satisfied
8. all of the alternatives
9. Does weight matter?

Part Four: In Class

Page 174, B. Listening and Note-Taking

Exercise 3

Lecturer: On the one hand, obviously, advertisers are in favor of product placement. Now why? Why? Well, because it works! Right? It sells products! It works.

For consumers—that's you and me, the people who watch the shows or read the books—there's another argument in support of product placement, and that is that it makes these stories more realistic. In real life people <u>do</u> drink Coke, right? You don't see them holding a can that just says "soda" or "soft drink," right? In some cases it would just look really strange or completely unbelievable not to use a name-brand product.

OK. Now, on the other hand there are some serious arguments against product placement. And the main argument, according to people who oppose it, is that it exposes us to advertising against our will. It's not like a television commercial where we have the choice of walking away or changing channels. With product placement the product's part of the story, so we're forced to see it.

Page 175, Exercise 5

Lecturer: Today we're going to talk about a form of advertising known as product placement, and I think the best way to explain this method of advertising is by looking at an example. Now before we started I asked you to look at a photo . . . and in this photo we see a man and a woman sitting at a table, talking, and there's this computer in front of them. Yeah? So how many of you thought this photo was a scene from a television program? OK. And how many thought it was an advertisement? Good. And how many of you thought it was both?

Wow. Yeah, if you said both, you were right. Yes. This is a scene from a popular American TV show called *24*. And this program is shown without any commercials, which is not very typical, but yeah, no commercials for this show. But did you notice what kind of computer the man is typing on? An Apple, yes. Yes. And do you think it's a coincidence that he's using an Apple and not some other computer brand? Of course not. Right. It's probably . . . the Apple computer company paid the producers of the show to "plant" their computer in this scene. This is what we mean by product placement. It is the practice of mentioning, using, or showing a brand-name product in a movie, film, or any other medium, so that the product actually becomes part of the story or the action. Now, it isn't a commercial, but it is advertising.

Now you can find examples of product placement in almost any medium. I've already mentioned television, and . . . How many of you here remember *Friends*? Yes, huge hit. Lots and lots of examples of product placement in this series. I'll just give you one example. There is a well-known scene where the character named Ross is sitting at the kitchen table with a package of Oreo cookies clearly visible. Um hmm.

Now in movies there are countless examples of product placement. And one of the absolute most famous examples of this is the BMW Z8 driven by James Bond in the movie *The World Is Not Enough*. All right. You can probably think of other examples of product placement involving cars; almost every movie includes some kind of example of this. It's like a soft drink, or . . . and if it's a soft drink, it's either Coke or Pepsi. Yeah? You get the picture. Good.

Product placement is most common in television and movies, but it's also easy to find in video games, pop songs, and even in books. Yes, books. I was shocked to find the name of this popular candy in the title of a book that teaches children how to count. But as product placement has become more and more common, it's also become more controversial. OK. Now, there are strong arguments both for and against it.

On the one hand, obviously, advertisers are in favor of product placement. Now why? Why? Well, because it works! Right? It sells products! It works. Now here's a famous example. There's a classic children's movie called *E.T.*, right? You've all seen it, about this cute space alien that makes friends with a young boy. And do you remember the alien's favorite food? It's a kind of candy called Reese's Pieces. Well, as soon as that movie came out, sales of Reese's Pieces went up by 65 percent. Now, eh, similarly, when you see Tom Cruise or any of those superstar guys wearing Ray Ban sunglasses or driving a certain kind of car, you can be sure that sales of those products are going to increase dramatically.

For consumers—that's you and me, the people who watch the shows or read the books—there's another argument in support of product placement, and that is that it makes these stories more realistic. In real life people do drink Coke, right? You don't see them holding a can that just says "soda" or "soft drink," right? In some cases it would just look really strange or completely unbelievable not to use a name-brand product.

OK. Now, on the other hand there are some serious arguments against product placement. And the main argument, according to people who oppose it, is that it exposes us to advertising against our will. It's not like a television commercial where we have the choice of walking away or changing channels. With product placement the product's part of the story, so we're forced to see it. And what's even worse, opponents say, is that sometimes the product placement is so clever, so subtle, we don't even realize that we're seeing an advertisement. Children, in particular, they may have a very difficult time understanding the difference between advertising and entertainment. And this was proven in a recent study at Lancaster University in England.

As a result of this research, some consumer groups are pushing for laws to restrict or even ban product placement in media designed for children. This may happen in the future, but for now, product placement is legal in both the U.S. and Great Britain and, in fact, it is expanding all the time.

CHAPTER EIGHT: DO THE RIGHT THING

Part One: In Person

Page 181, B. Listening

Exercise 1

David: I've actually heard a lot of interesting ways that people have cheated. One way is, um, basically when they're asked to write an essay, they, um. . .and they need like a fifteen-page paper, and they, and by the time they need to turn it in they only had seven pages. So what they did was, they ended the seventh page mid-sentence, and they numbered the pages, and basically turned it in and they ended up getting an e-mail from their professor back saying "Oh, I must have lost your last couple of pages, can you get them in to me?" So basically they had an extension for another couple of days to finish their paper.

Ilana: That's crazy.

Nira: Yeah, I've heard of that a lot.

I: Sometimes also if you know that a teacher is going to hand back an exam, like an essay before the lecture ends, some people just never hand it in and then wait until the teacher hands back essays and say "Wait! You never handed me mine." And then the professor looks all confused and says, "Oh, I never got your essay." And then you could say "Are you serious? Like I've turned it in to you. Like I'll email it—I'll email it to you tonight." I've like. . .I think that's happened before.

Lida: What about some of these high-tech ways of cheating. People somehow transmit the answers to each other, things like that, are you, have you heard of anything of that sort?

D: I know that in one of my classes, we were told of the possibility of having an open laptop test. . .was going to happen during my programming class. And I heard people talking about how, since we have wireless Internet, they could go on Instant Messenger and IM each other the correct answers.

I: That's really smart. Really wrong, but very smart. It's like "genius" cheating.

L: Given that, have you ever been tempted? Would you ever do it?

D: No, I'm never tempted to cheat.

I: Give me a break. Come on, you've been tempted to cheat before. None of us are perfect.

D: No, me, never.

I: I think you're pulling my leg. Come on. Be honest with us.

D: I'm not. I've never cheated.

I: Let's say you were so stressed out, you had studied really hard, you had gotten no sleep, and then you got to the test, and this was like a test that determined whether you were going to get an A in that class or an F. Like there are tests that are sometimes worth almost like 60 percent of your grade. And then you saw that test and you totally blanked on all the information. And you knew that this person sitting next to you was a straight-A student who definitely knew all the answers. You wouldn't be tempted to cheat?

D: I wouldn't cheat because I would feel morally wrong.

I: David, I don't believe you for one second.

D: I might consider it, but I probably wouldn't. Well, what would you do?

I: Um, I'd say, if it was like the scenario I described, I don't know if I would cheat or not, but I would definitely be tempted to if I was in that situation. And I think you would be too.

D: I'll agree. I'd probably be tempted.

I: What about you?

N: Honestly? I would definitely cheat. I mean, come on. Getting an F? Or just looking over at a straight-A student's test and, you know, seeing the answers and getting a good grade. . . Who wants to get an F?

Page 181, Exercise 2. Repeat the recording from Exercise 1.

Page 184, Exercise 7

Young Woman: Most people would lie in order to save a life, but they wouldn't do it to save money. What would you do? For example, would you steal food if you were hungry and poor? I would understand if you said yes. But the police wouldn't be so kind. What would your mom and dad do if you got arrested? They would help you, wouldn't they? But they wouldn't be proud of you.

Part Two: On the Phone

Page 189, B. Listening

Exercise 1

Taped Message: Thank you for calling the university police department Lost and Found. We are currently away from our desk. If you have lost an item on campus, you may leave a message after the tone. The message should include your name, a telephone number, and a brief description of the item. We will return your call only if we receive the item. Please note: Keys and sunglasses are kept at the front desk of the police department. If you have lost one of these items, you must come to the station in person to check for them. If you are calling to report a found object, you may bring the item directly to the station. The police station is located at 6104 South Circle Drive, one block north of Sunnyfield Plaza. To leave a message, please wait for the tone. To speak to someone in the lost and found department, please press zero.

University Police Officer: Lost and Found, can I help you?

Caller: Uh, hi. Um, I found a watch and I was wondering if anyone called in about it?

UPO: Okay, what kind of watch?

C: It's a men's Rolex. Did anyone call in about it?

UPO: Well, I'm going to have to check on that. In the meantime, I can take down your name and number, and we'll call you if anybody reports it missing.

C: Uh-huh.

UPO: Or of course you can bring it in at any time to our station and drop it off at the front desk.

C: Yeah, well, actually. . . I was wondering if there was a reward for it.

UPO: Ah. We don't actually give out any information about rewards. That would be against university policy.

C: Hum, well, if I bring it in and nobody claims it? Then can I keep it?

UPO: Well, the university policy says, once you turn in an object you can contact us after ninety days to check if anyone has claimed it. If not, then you're entitled to keep it. Those items that haven't been claimed after ninety days are donated to charity.

C: OK.

UPO: But we would certainly encourage you to do the right thing and bring in any object you find that doesn't belong to you.

C: Yeah, well, I'll, I'll think it over.

UPO: OK, thank you for calling.

C: OK. Bye-bye.

UPO: Bye.

Page 190, Exercise 2. Repeat the recording from Exercise 1.

Part Three: On the Air

Page 195, B. Listening

Exercise 1

Interviewer: Dr. Feldman?

Dr. Feldman: Hi.

I: Hi. How are you?

Dr. F.: I'm doing well, thanks. How are you?

I: Good. And I really mean it.

Dr. F.: So do I.

I: Good. All right, now, are you really saying that we're all lying all the time?

Dr. F.: What I'm saying is that we lie a lot more than we think we do. And that everyday social interactions are filled with lies.

I: Now, how did you come to this conclusion? I mean your specific statistics: sixty percent of us tell a lie at least once in a ten-minute conversation?

Dr. F.: Well, no, I wouldn't say it that way. We ran a study in which we asked people to get to know another person. And we let them talk with one another for ten minutes. And then we asked them to review a videotape that we made of them while they were, uh, interacting with one another. What we found was that. . .

I: And then you asked when they told the truth?

Dr. F.: We asked them when they said anything that was not entirely accurate.

I: OK.

Dr. F.: And what we found was that 60 percent of those people lied at least once. The mean number of lies was three and some people lied as much as twelve times during that ten-minute period.

I: Twelve times? About what?

Dr. F.: Uh, just about anything. Some people lied about very mundane things, trying to make the person they were talking to feel better. Other people lied about where they'd been, who they were, accomplishments; it really ranged the gamut.

I: Well, in terms of making people feel better, you mean things like "I really like your hair"? "That's a great shirt"?

Dr. F.: Yeah, "I really like this movie. How about you?" "Oh, yes, I really like that movie, too." In fact, they didn't like the movie or they hadn't seen the movie even.

I: Right. But they're just trying to be friends.

Dr. F.: They were just trying to be friendly. And actually, that was one of the big differences we found between men and women. Although men and women lied at about the same rate, women tended to lie to make the person they were talking to feel better about themselves. Men. . .

I: Or to ingratiate themselves.

Dr. F.: Or to ingratiate themselves.

I: Yeah.

Dr. F.: But men tended to lie more about themselves. They built themselves up; they said they had accomplishments that they really did not.

I: Oh, that's typical, isn't it? Was that a surprise to you?

Dr. F.: It was a surprise to me, but it's not a surprise to a lot of women I know.

I: That's right.

Page 196, Exercise 2. Repeat the recording from Exercise 1.

Part Four: In Class

Page 202, B. Listening and Note-Taking

Exercise 2

1. OK, earlier we talked about the definition of an ethical dilemma. We said that it's a situation where you're forced to make a choice that involves your beliefs about right and wrong behavior. Now I think most people know the difference between right and wrong, and I think most people, when they find themselves in a situation where there is a clear difference between right and wrong, they will choose to do the right thing. But what happens when the choice isn't between a right action and a wrong action but between two actions that are both right?

2. Suppose your good friend is dressing in a way that's unattractive or unprofessional. Um, it's the wrong color, uh, it doesn't fit, or whatever. Do you tell your friend the truth, that the outfit looks bad because you want to be helpful, or do you keep quiet because you don't want to hurt your friend's feelings?

Page 202, Exercise 4

Lecturer: Suppose you work for a company that makes plastic toys. And you discover that your company is spilling dangerous chemicals into a river nearby. Should you report the company to the government in order to protect the people who live near the factory, or should you keep quiet in order to protect yourself and keep your job? You can't do both! Uh, by the way, this is exactly what happens in the movie *Erin Brockovich,* um, if anyone has seen it. Erin Brockovich, uh, who's played by Julia Roberts, is a secretary who discovers that the gas company is poisoning the people of the town where she lives and of course they're trying to hide it, and she has to decide whether to make this public or keep quiet in order to protect her reputation and her job. And I'm sure you can guess what happens at the end of the movie. Anyway, so those are some examples, then, of the self versus community dilemma.

Page 203, Exercise 5

Lecturer: OK, earlier we talked about the definition of an ethical dilemma… We said that it's a situation where you're forced to make a choice that involves your beliefs about right and wrong behavior. Now I think most people know the difference between right and wrong, and I think most people, when they find themselves in a situation where there is a clear difference between what's right and wrong, they will choose to do the right thing. But what happens when the choice isn't between a right action and a wrong action but between two actions that are both right? This is something that we all face in our lives from time to time, isn't it? So today I want to look at three types of these right versus right dilemmas, um we'll look at some examples, and later I'll ask you to think about what you might do if you were in these situations. OK?

OK, so the first type of dilemma I want to describe is something I'm sure you've encountered in your own life. It's called a truth versus loyalty dilemma. Let's suppose that you have a good friend who is using drugs. OK, and you know about it but your friend has asked you not to tell anyone. This immediately creates a dilemma for you, doesn't it? On the one hand your friend asked you not to tell anybody. So you can be a loyal friend and agree to keep his secret.

But the problem is, drugs are dangerous. Drugs are illegal. Your friend could die, right? So do you keep quiet and keep your friend's secret or do you tell somebody, such as his parents, and get him the help that he needs? You see both actions are good and correct by themselves, but you can't do both. You have to choose. So what do you do?

Or here's another example, um a simpler one. Suppose your good friend is dressing in a way that's unattractive or unprofessional. Um, it's the wrong color, uh, it doesn't fit, or whatever. Do you tell your friend the truth, that the outfit looks bad because you want to be helpful, or do you keep quiet because you don't want to hurt your friend's feelings? Again, it's a situation where both choices are ethically correct, but you can only choose to do one. OK? So those are two examples of the truth versus loyalty dilemma.

Another type of dilemma is called the self versus community dilemma. And here there is a conflict between the needs or desires of one person and the needs or desires of a larger group such as your family, or your class, or your town, or even your country. Let's say that your parents want you to become a doctor. They think it's the best thing for you and of course it would make them happy. But you don't want to be a doctor. You want to be an artist. So you have a dilemma. On the one hand, you want to please your parents. But on the other hand, you want to please yourself, and you can't do both. Does this sound familiar?

Or here's another example, um, the kind of thing that you read about in the newspaper every day. Suppose you work for a company that makes plastic toys. And you discover that your company is spilling dangerous chemicals into a river nearby. Should you report the company to the government in order to protect the people who live near the factory, or should you keep quiet in order to protect yourself and keep your job? You can't do both! Uh, by the way, this is exactly what happens in the movie *Erin Brockovich*, um, if anyone has seen it. Erin Brockovich, uh, who's played by Julia Roberts, is a secretary who discovers that the gas company is poisoning the people of the town where she lives and of course they're trying to hide it, and she has to decide whether to make this public or keep quiet in order to protect her reputation and her job. And I'm sure you can guess what happens at the end of the movie. Anyway, so those are some examples, then, of the self versus community dilemma.

All right, the third type of dilemma I want to describe is also something I'm sure you have had to face in your own life. What we have here is a conflict between short-term and long-term needs or goals. So if you're seven years old, the dilemma might be should you eat all your candy now or save some for later? At age sixteen

it might be should you spend your money on a car now or should you save it to pay for college later? And at the national level, the dilemma might be, um should a government keep taxes low in order to be popular in the short term with voters, or should it raise taxes in order to pay for new universities that will be needed five years from now? This is the kind of dilemma, incidentally, that the United States government faces all of the time because of the nature of the political system that we have here. So in all of these examples, what you see is a conflict between the needs or desires of the present as opposed to the needs or desires of the future. Both choices have certain advantages, but it's only possible to choose one of them.

So by now I think you can begin to understand that ethical dilemmas are not easy to resolve. Yet life is full of hard choices, isn't it, so wouldn't it be useful if there were some strategies or guidelines we could use to think through our ethical dilemmas and make the right choices? Well, that is exactly the topic we're going to examine next.